The Story of Hungarian
A GUIDE TO THE LANGUAGE

D1548267

Translated by
THOMAS J. DEKORNFELD

GÉZA BALÁZS

The Story of Hungarian

A GUIDE TO THE LANGUAGE

CORVINA

I wish to thank the following persons for the invaluable
assistance they offered me in writing this book:
DR. ERZSÉBET BEÖTHY (UvA, Amsterdam),
DR. PÁL FÁBIÁN (ELTE, Budapest),
DR. LÁSZLÓ MARÁCZ (UvA, Amsterdam, Alphen a/d Ryn),
and MÁRIA GEDEON (Eötvös College, Budapest).

Consultant
DR. MIHÁLY HAJDÚ (ELTE, Budapest)

Copyright © GÉZA BALÁZS, 1997

English translation © THOMAS J. DEKORNFELD

On the cover: *Allegory of the Sciences and the Arts*
(1820), by Pál Balkay
(National Gallery, Budapest)

Published by Corvina Books, Ltd.
Budapest V., Vörösmarty tér 1, Hungary 1051

This volume has been published with support from the
Magyar Könyv Alapítvány
and the *Frankfurt '99 Programiroda*

ISBN 963 13 4362 6

Table of Contents

"Are you aware that there is a language that because of its constructive ability and the harmony of its rhythm I have placed on the same level as Greek and Latin? It is the Hungarian language! I know the poems of the new Hungarian poets and their music has completely enchanted me. Keep your eye on future developments and you will witness such an upsurge in poetic genius, which will totally justify my prediction. It seems the Hungarians themselves are ignorant of the treasure concealed within their language."

CARDINAL GIUSEPPE MEZZOFANTI, 1774-1849
in: Watts Transactions of the Phylological Society, 1855.

Foreword

According to an old story, everybody in Debrecen – perhaps the most important city on the Great Hungarian Plain – is a physician. In this city, every person who feels poorly gets medical advice from every acquaintance. Naturally these are usually contradictory and often mutually exclusive. It is also believed that in Hungary everybody is a poet. This is what the editors of literary magazines have said for a hundred years in view of the deluge of poetry submitted to them. Most of it is doggerel, some of it is genius.

It is easy to see why everybody in Hungary is a linguist as well. People are generally aware of the fact that the Hungarian language is peculiar and thus they all try to make themselves understood in their own peculiar way. Everybody knows one or two linguistic superstitions (naive linguistic advice), and is ready to criticize every other person's use of the language. To be involved in linguistic matters and to be deeply involved in the intricacies of the language is a national preoccupation.

Those who become acquainted with Hungary and thus with the Hungarian language will notice a number of other things: the Hungarian loves his belly, loves to drink, tell tales and dance. He will keep his guests entertained and is familiar with many sayings, proverbs and quotations. There are books in every apartment.

Language is the principal characteristic of an ethnic group and the most important guarantee for the ongoing inheritance of its traditions. Learning about the several thousand year old Hungarian language, one of the "ancient" languages in Europe, would be of benefit to all who wish to encounter, here in the middle of Europe, a distinctly different language and culture.

Those who become acquainted with this language and culture will learn about Asia, Europe and European history. It is not a "small" language. Considering the number of people speaking Hungarian, this language takes the 47th place among all the languages in the world and the 12th place among the 67 languages spoken in Europe. It is the community of 15 million people speaking the same language who address the reader in the pages of this little book.

The Hungarians and Hungary (Pannonia)

The Hungarians call themselves Magyars and their land Magyarország, but in most other languages they are styled differently. The international designation of the country is "H" and this is what appears on the license plates of the cars and in the letter code for mail from outside Hungary. "H" is also the mark of Hungarian money: "HUF" (Hungarian Forint). The "H" designation for Hungary was derived from the medieval Latin *hungarus*. From 700 A.D. on, the word *hungarus* appears about 60 times in Carolingian charters. Magyarország is called Hungary in English, *Vengrija* in Russian, *Węgry* in Polish, *Ungarn* in German, *Hongrie* in French, *Ungheria* in Italian, and only in the neighboring Slovakian *Madarsko* is there any similarity to the original.

Whence do these foreign designations come which use the syllables *veng-, hung-, ung-*, etc. as the introductory sound to the name? The original source of these names is the Turkish name for the nation: *onogur*, which means *on* (ten) *ogur* (arrows), an ancient tribal designation. The Onogurs are first mentioned in the 5th century. There were several tribes called *ogur* living between the Dnyeper and the Volga during the 5th-9th centuries. The ancestors of the Hungarians lived with these tribes and were therefore also called Onogurs.

The Ugor designation is thus derived from the Turkic national name Onogur, and it is from here that the Slavic names for the Hungarians are derived (e.g. the Czech *Uhersky*, Polish *Węgierski* and Russian *Ugirskij*). Starting probably with the 7th century and under the influence of Latin, the terms *Ungarus - Hungarus* spread to the West.

The initial "H" in the western European names for the Magyars, such as the English *Hungarian* and the French

Hongrois comes from identifying the Hungarians with the Huns. Thus the Hungarian-Hun associations appear as early as the 7th century.

The Huns, who were a nomadic equestrian people probably speaking some Turkic language and originating from Central-Asia appeared in the Carpathian Basin for the first time in the 5th century and were the first ones to establish a strong empire in this region. They withdrew toward the East after 455 A.D. The Hunor and Magor legend appearing in medieval Hungarian chronicles hints strongly at the common origin of the Huns and the Hungarians.

Nations usually referred to themselves simply as "people". Magyar is a composite word of which the first part may have sounded like *mogy* - and referred to a national designation from the Ugor period and *eri*, meaning "man, male". The first time the composite word *mogyeri* appears is in 810.

The word appeared in several forms in several sources. We have *magyar* and *megyer*. The phonetically higher ("thinner" front vowel) *megyer* variation might have referred to something smaller and may have been the name of one of the conquering Hungarian tribes. To this date we have place-names giving clear indication of the areas settled by the Megyer tribe, such as north of Budapest: *Békásmegyer, Káposztásmegyer* and also *Megyer, Bábonymegyer, Nagymegyer, Nógrádmegyer, Pócsmegyer,* etc. The deeper ("fatter" back vowel) word *Magyar* became the internal national name of the Hungarians, being the second tonal modification of the name of the largest and most dominant tribe.

About half of present-day Hungary: Transdanubia (= *Dunántúl*), with Croatia and Slovenia formed the Roman province called Pannonia. The border (*limes*) ran along the banks of the Danube. The original Illyrian meaning of the word pannon was swamp or mud and the province probably derived its name from the area surrounding Lake Balaton. Hungarian historians are very much aware of the Pannonian-Hungarian traditions and the medieval humanists, under Latin (Italian) influence, started calling Hungary Pannonia again. The names of certain tools and processes used in viniculture, place names and road names (e.g. *Borostyánkő út* - Amber Way) are very ancient and indicate a close contact between the descendants of the former Pannonian inhabitants and the conquering Hungarians. Pécs (*Sopianae* in Roman times) was one of the centers of early Christian culture. In Fenékpuszta (*Valcum* in Roman times), near Lake Balaton, the archaeologists discovered an early Christian basilica. The agriculturists living in this area were assimilated and carried over viniculture from the Romans to the Hungarians.

Of the approximately 130 Latin place names of ancient Pannonia relatively few survived the age of the great migrations since the Huns and Avars who settled here spoke no Latin. But even so, *Danuvius* = Danube, *Dravus* = Dráva, *Savus* = Száva, *Arrabo* = Rába, *Mursella* = Marcal, *Salla* = Zala, *Granua* = Garam did survive. The similarity between the Pannonian name Vindobona and the current Austrian name Wien for the same city is striking. The city of Paks, lying along the Danubian border and "boasting" Hungary's first and only atomic power plant, appears in some very early writings as *Pax* and *Paxi*, after "peace", which suggests that this was a Latin name as well.

Several other Pannonian towns had their old name revived again and a number of them are used quite regularly in present day Hungary: Győr = *Arrabona*, Sopron = *Scarbantia*, Szombathely = *Savaria* (with the famous Isis-shrine), Pécs = *Sopianae*, Szőny = *Brigetio*, Óbuda = *Aquincum*, Tác = *Gorsium*, etc.

The Latin traditions of the area contributed to the partial Latinization (Indo-Europeanization) of the Hungarian language from the 10th century onward.

13

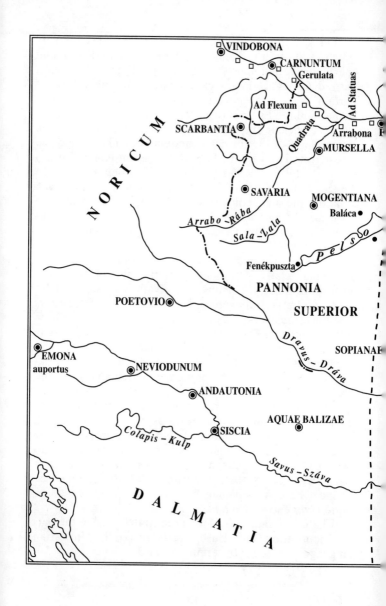

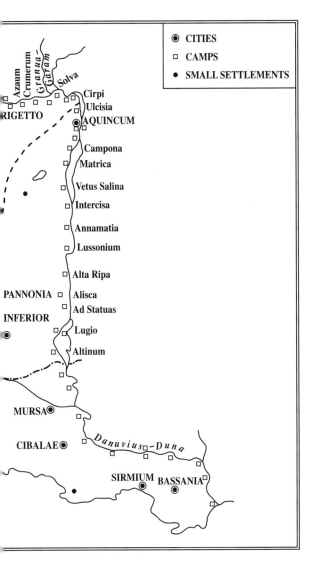

Figure 1. The Latin place names of the Roman Age

The Hungarian Language in the World

The approximately six billion people living on our planet speak at least 3,000 different languages. The ten most widely spoken languages, used by about half of the world's population, are: Chinese, English, Hindi, Spanish, Arabic, Bengali, Portuguese, Indonesian, Japanese and Russian. There are another 48 languages which may be classified as major, since they are spoken by more than 10 million people. Considering that about 15 million people speak Hungarian, this puts the language among the top 50 and, according to one calculation it is the 47th.

In Europe today, between the Atlantic Ocean and the Urals, 67 languages are spoken and among these Hungarian ranks 12th on the basis of the number of people for whom it is the native language. Of the 22 so-called national languages, Hungarian stands again 12th. The rank-order of the European languages, based on the number of people who speak the language, is: German, Russian, English, Italian, French, Ukrainian, Spanish, Dutch, Portuguese and Hungarian. Very close behind Hungarian are Serbian, Bielorussian, Greek and Bulgarian.

This obviously does not mean that the number of people speaking a language, in any way determine the relative importance of that language or of the people speaking it. In Europe there are a number of "small languages" which constitute a European "linguistic museum". Were they to die out, the world would be the poorer for it.

The position of the Hungarian language is a very peculiar one because the 1920 Trianon Peace Treaty (imposed by the Great Powers) dismembered Hungary and today in East-Central-Europe (i.e., in the eastern part of Central Europe), Hungarian is spoken in eight countries in addition to Hungary. One of the largest national blocks lives in

Romania – the Transylvanian Hungarians. These nationalities are usually referred to as minorities, although in this case in sizable areas the Hungarians make up a significant majority over the representatives of the so-called national state. According to the most conservative estimates, the number of Hungarians living in Romania is put at 2 million. In Slovakia, reasonably accurate estimates put the number at 750,000. There is a significant Hungarian population in the Ukraine (Kárpátalja), Lesser Yugoslavia (Vajdaság), fewer in Croatia (Slavonia and the Szerémség), Slovenia, Austria and very few in the Czech Republic. This means that in the areas adjacent to present-day Hungary, Hungarian is spoken in the cities and villages, or, rather, that Hungarian is spoken there as well. To this number we must add the mixed marriages where after some time the marriage partner is likely to know at least some Hungarian.

There are numerous statistics about the number of Hungarians. It is extremely difficult to cite a precise number, since numbering techniques vary, national belonging may change and there may be major population shifts. Because of Romanian domestic politics, tens of thousands of Transylvanian Hungarians fled to Hungary during the 1980s. During the fighting in Yugoslavia (1992-1995) more than ten thousand Hungarians settled permanently or temporarily in Hungary. There is a well-known story from Kárpátalja, near the Hungarian-Ukrainian border: A Hungarian in the Kárpátalja was asked how many different countries he had seen during his life. He thought for a moment and then said: "Five. And all of them without leaving my city." Until 1920, the Kárpátalja belonged to Hungary (Austro-Hungarian Monarchy), until 1938 to Czechoslovakia, then again to Hungary, one part to the independent Slovakia, and from 1947 to the Soviet Union. Since 1990 and at the present time it belongs to the Ukraine. The Hungarians living beyond Hungary proudly say:

"We have not crossed the border, the border has crossed us."

Census figures rarely reveal the true ethnic-linguistic conditions. The following tables for 1969 and 1980 were compiled by Zoltán Dávid, the historian-ethnographer. The third column gives the estimates made by the Hungarian World Federation in 1996.

	1969	1980	Jan. 1996
Hungary	9,900,000	10,000,000	10,100,000
Austria	50,000	70,000	50,000
Czechoslovakia	730,000	750,000	–
		Czech Rep	20,000
		Slovakia	700,000
Soviet Union	170,000	200,000	
		Russia	20,000
		Ukraine	200,000
Romania	1,850,000	2,000,000	2,000,000
Yugoslavia	550,000	450,000	
		Lesser Yugoslavia	400,000
		Croatia	25,000
		Slovenia	15,000
Germany	50,000	50,000	50,000
France	50,000	35,000	35,000
Belgium	5,000	10,000	10,000
U.K.	25,000	10,000	40,000
Italy	10,000	10,000	5,000
Switzerland	15,000	10,000	20,000
Netherlands	10,000	5,000	5,000
Other E.U.Countries	15,000	10,000	n.a.

Total: Western Europe   **250,000**

United States	800,000	600,000	650,000
Canada	100,000	100,000	150,000
Brazil	60,000	40,000	100,000
Argentina	15,000	15,000	n.a.
Other American	15,000	5,000	n.a.

Total South and Central America: **100,000**

Total The Americas: **1,000,000**

Australia	35,000	50,000	45,000
Oceania			5,000
Africa	5,000	5,000	20,000*

*Of these 5,000 in the Republic of South Africa

Asia	20,000	20,000	230,000
		(Israel:	200,000)
Total			
in the World	14,500,000	14,500,000	15,150,000

Some complementary data:

Hungary (on the basis of the 1990 census): Population - 10,381,959 of whom on the basis of native language 10,222,529 were Hungarian, 48,072 Gypsy, 35,511 German, 17,577 Croatian, 12,745 Slovakian, 2,953 Serb, 2,627 Slovenian and 22,079 other.

Romania (on the basis of the 1992 census): Hungarian and Székely nationals 1,620,199. They considered the Hungarians, the Székelys and the Csángós as separate nationalities, although they are all Hungarians, and did not publish native language data which have always showed more Hungarians in all previous Romanian censuses than suggested by the nationality data.

Slovakia (on the basis of the 1991 census in the Slovakian part of Czechoslovakia): 566,741 persons listed themselves as Hungarian nationals (20,143 in the Czech part). The Hungarian nationals constituted 11% of the population of Slovakia.

In evaluating these numbers some additional factors must be taken into consideration. The number of births is decreasing in Hungary and thus the population is slowly decreasing. During recent years, this decrease was compensated for by Hungarians moving back from the neighboring countries, but this decreased the number of Hungarians beyond the borders. Since the various countries use different statistical methods, there is no concordance in the measurements and the final numbers must be viewed critically. It may also be observed that due to political and historic influences, in certain countries there may be a spectacular "growth" or "decrease" in the number of a given nationality. There are some very peculiar communities which consider themselves Hungarian and having a Hungarian identity. There is a village both in Switzerland and in France where the inhabitants claim to be of Hun-Hungarian descent. Several Caucasian people (Chechen and Uigur) maintain a kinship with Hungary. In Egypt, on the Sudan border, there is a 7,000 member community which is called *Magyarab* (Hung-Arab). They maintain their Hungarian identity and their Christian heritage. In Turkey there are four villages identified as Hungarian. In Israel (Galilee) there are two Arab villages near the city of Nahrija (one is called *Magar*) where the inhabitants have largely Hungarian given names. It is the assumption that they are descendants of the crusaders of King Endre II, who had settled here. The inhabitants of these villages bear little physical resemblance to the residents of the neighboring Arab villages.

Taking into account all these factors, one usually talks about 15 million Hungarians of whom one third lives beyond the borders of Hungary.

The Hungarian language is the official language of Hungary, but Hungarian as a means of communication can be used in many other countries as well. The Hungarian nationals, living in other countries, can use Hungarian in different ways and to a different degree. There are countries where there is instruction in Hungarian from grade school to the university, and there are many places where we can see Hungarian inscriptions, newspapers, books, radio and television programs.

The First Hungarian World Congress was organized in 1929. The Hungarian World Federation, encompassing all Hungarians, was formed in 1938, in commemoration of the 900th anniversary of the death of St. Stephen. Since 1992, the short-wave programs of Radio Kossuth, and (the mostly cultural) programs of Duna Television can be heard and seen, in Hungarian, in all of Europe and much of the Middle East. Since 1996 programs of the Hungarian Radio can also be heard through the Internet. At the present time, Hungarian language and literature (including history and ethnography) is taught in about 100 universities in approximately 25 countries.

Considering its geographic spread, Hungarian belongs among the more modest languages. Until the Turkish occupation (16th c.), the Carpathian Basin was largely inhabited by Hungarians. After this time their number shrunk to about 40%. A solid (connected, closed) Hungarian population lives in the entire area of present Hungary and on the other side of the borders in the north, northeast and south. In this overall area approximately 12-12.5 million Hungarians live as a block. The dissemination of the Hungarian language within Hungary is complete and homogenous. The other connected, compact block is the Székelyföld (in the middle of Romania, the southeastern part of Transylania) where approximately 900,000 Hungarians live. In the Székelyföld, in County Hargita the ratio of Hungarians is 85% and in County Kovászna it is 75%. Even in County Maros the percentage of Hungarians is as high as 41%.

The remaining groups of Hungarians in the Carpathian Basin live in smaller or larger scattered linguistic islands. Such a linguistic island is the Transylvanian Kalotaszeg (with forty settlements including Kalotaszentkirály, Körös-fő and Alsóőr), and there are other smaller Transylvanian settlements. They appear also in the Mezőség, in the Austrian Burgenland around Felsőőr (Felsőőr, Őrsziget, Alsóőr), and in the Hungarian islands in Croatia and Slavonia which survived even the Turkish occupation, but of which three villages near Eszék were totally destroyed during the recent Yugoslavian civil war.

Outside of the Carpathian Basin, there is a *Csángó* linguistic island in Moldavia (Romania). The Moldavian Hungarians live between the eastern Carpathians and the Pruth river and settled here in the 13th century from the Maros district of Transylvania. According to other historians, they have been there since the original migration. They have been bilingual for a very long time and a large percentage have become assimilated Romanians (Romanian politicians occasionally refer to them as "Magyarized Romanians"). Their origin is strongly supported by the fact that they are Roman Catholics. At the end of the 1940s - at the time of Petru Groza's Prime Ministership - the Moldavian Csángó had a Hungarian Teacher's College, 100 schools, and 13 kindergartens. Today the Csángó have not even a single one of these. They are not allowed to hear Hungarian even in church and they do not appear in the census. Anybody, however, who knows Hungarian and is familiar with old Hungarian usage, when listening to the Csángó, fancies that he is listening to Hungarian spoken 500 years ago. According to the best estimate, their number can be put at 40-60 thousand.

The most eventful history is that of the Bukovina Székelys. A small Hungarian linguistic island was established here in 1777 by a few thousand Székelys who were trying to escape the arbitrary oppression of the Habsburg border guards. At the end of the last century most of them were resettled in Transylvania and along the lower reaches of the Danube. In 1941, the Hungarian government moved them to the Bácska, to the south of Hungary. Many of them fell victim there to the Serb massacres at the end

22

of 1944. Approximately 13,000 escaped and after the end of World War II, settled again in Hungary, mostly in Counties Tolna, Baranya, Bács and Pest. The largest groups are in Kakasd, Hidas and Érd where they preserve their ancient traditions, stories and customs to this day.

Approximately 600,000 Hungarians live in the United States, mostly in New York City, Cleveland, Los Angeles, Chicago, Detroit, Pittsburgh and Philadelphia. According to the 1980 census, 1.7 million people in the U.S. claimed to be of Hungarian descent and 178,995 reported that they were speaking Hungarian at home.

Public opinion and the facts are not in accord: the Hungarian language in Europe is not a small language, and for historic reasons it still serves as a lingua franca and communication link in the Carpathian Basin and in Central-Europe.

A Hungarian ethnographer at the end of the 19th century put it very well when he said: *"Hungary is Europe in miniature."* It could even be said that Hungary was Eurasia in miniature.

Hungarian popular culture is a link between East and West. The Carpathian Basin and the history of the Hungarians living therein are a veritable treasure house of all conceivable linguistic-cultural connections, from incidental contacts, through a symbiotic exchange of influences, to complete assimilation. This is shown by the traditions of Hungarian music, folklore, architecture, agriculture, and even cuisine. The Hungarians absorbed the culturally similar and genetically not distinguishable Avars and western and southern Slavs. They also assimilated the Saxons, the northern Italian Walloons, the eastern Alanian-Jazygians, the Cumanians and other Turkic fragments and, later, the Germans and the Slovakians and the majority of the Gypsies and of the Jews.

The Hungarians are the largest Finno-Ugrian people, having the oldest written language, and living farthest south. At the same time, they are the farthest northern people with traces of Turkish culture. They are also the farthest west from both their genetic-cultural "progenitors" (parents). Among the manifold cultural streams, changes and linguistic influences, the Hungarians have lost neither their identity, nor their language (a number of Finno-Ugrian, Turkic and Indo-European people and languages have died out). To accomplish this, they required openness, flexibility, and considerable adaptability.

The mementos of the early ages of the Carpathian Basin constitute a museum of collections, rich in archeologic, physiologic and ethnographic findings which all indicate a common Carpathian or Carpathian-Basin heritage.

In spite of, or because of this multiplicity of shades, the Hungarian language is unique in Europe. It is remarkably kinship-free, ancient, and unified. People living at any two most distant points of the Hungarian language area (as much as 600-700 km.) whose primary language may be different, can communicate with each other in Hungarian easily and without hindrance.

The Character of the Hungarian Language

Is Hungarian a difficult language?

It is the unanimous opinion of all foreigners, of those becoming acquainted with Hungarian, and of those trying to learn the language, that Hungarian is "tough". In general, of course, there are no easy or tough languages. It all depends on the learner's native tongue, on how many other languages he/she knows, how old he/she is and what motivates them to learn Hungarian. The Turks, for instance, don't claim that Hungarian is difficult – in Turkish bazaars and stores, the Hungarians are addressed in Hungarian with a Turkish accent (*"madjar"*), are given advertising leaflets (grammatically incorrect, but understandable), and can be reasonably well talked to, even though the Turks have not learned their Hungarian from textbooks, but from the streets. The situation is similar in several Austrian, northern Italian, Egyptian and Greek cities, resorts and "bazaars", wherever there are appreciable numbers of Hungarian tourists.

In the case of Western European students, the situation is quite different. For them, the Hungarian language seems difficult because, although they may speak several similar Indo-European languages, Hungarian differs markedly from all of them. For a Chinese or Vietnamese – thousands of whom have come to Hungary in recent years – the Hungarian language does not appear to be any more difficult than English or German. Even though Finnish is related to Hungarian, the Finns do not find Hungarian easy and, conversely, the Hungarians find Finnish to be a difficult language. This may be due to the fact that the two peoples and the two languages live in entirely different environments, and the kinship is evident only to linguists. The Hungarians have no obvious linguistic relatives. For a

Hollander neither English, German nor Friesean appears as very "foreign" languages. The average Hungarian would not even recognize Finnish or Estonian for what they are, even though linguistically they are related to Hungarian.

Hungarian should not be taken for more complicated than other languages. It seems tough only for those who have never encountered a language having a completely different structure than their own.

It has some linguistic characteristics, however, which make the Hungarian language relatively easy for the speaker of some Indo-European languages. Thus, for instance, the phonetic structure of Hungarian contains no particular sounds that can not be easily pronounced by a Frenchman, Italian, German or Englishman. Hungarian is written with Roman characters. Thus only the double letters (*cs, gy, sz, ty, ny, zs*) must be learned and they only represent a single sound. The Hungarian written language reflects the pronunciation more accurately than the French or the English one and, in this, it resembles the German. The accented vowels (*a-á, e-é*) may seem peculiar, but they are logical and rational.

Hungarian has the same principal parts of speech as the Indo-European languages. We have verbs, nouns, adjectives, numerals, pronouns, adverbs, articles, postpositions, conjunctions, particles and interjections. There are also verbal prefixes and participles. In the Hungarian sentence the dominant word is the verb. The most important part of the sentence, the predicate, is usually a verb (of course, it may be a noun also).

What is it that we do not have in the Hungarian language?

• There are no prepositions.

• There are no genders, which cause so much grief in other languages. There are no pronouns indicating gender. In the third person, there is only one gender (*ő*), which in English would have to be "he," "she," or "it".

•There is no single verb structure to mark the possessive.

•There is only a very limited use of passive conjugation. In conjugation in ordinary use there is only one single present, past, and future tense.

Even though the Finno-Ugrian and old Turkic elements in the Hungarian vocabulary are quite unique and not easy to learn for those speaking an Indo-European language, Hungarian does have a number of words of Latin, German, English and other extractions, as well as new words which have received a world-wide distribution (mostly English). These may be used in their original version or may be slightly modified but easily recognizable and thus the learner will not have to acquire a completely new vocabulary. The following sentences, heard regularly in conversation, should have a number of familiar elements:

A mai program: múzeum, koncert, opera; megyünk bankba és postára. (Today's program: museum, concert and opera; we are going to the bank and to the post office.)

A Bankpont automatánál használhatjuk a kreditkártyát. (At the bank automatic service we can use a credit card).

Hívj föl telefonon. (Call me on the telephone.)

Faxold át ezt a papírt. (Fax me that paper.)

Magyarország az Európai Unió tagja akar lenni. (Hungary wishes to become a member of the European Union.)

Autóval vagy Intercityvel menjek Miskolcra? (Should I go to Miskolc by car or by the Intercity train?)

Egy hot-dogot ettem a McDonald'sban. (I ate a hot-dog at McDonald's.)

Magyarország europaizálódik vagy balkanizálódik? (Is Hungary becoming Europeanized or Balkanized?)

Biciklizem a parkban. Az autóm itt parkol. (I am bicycling in the park. My car is parked here.)

Víkendezni mentem, vittem magammal pulóvert, teát, kávét és kakaót. (I went away for a weekend and took a pullover, tea, coffee and cocoa.)

Randevúm van a diszkóban. (I have a rendezvous at the disco).

We do not claim that all Hungarian sentences will be this familiar, but we do say that among the many unknown forms and words we will meet many "familiar" forms.

The greatest difference in sentence structure is that in Hungarian the individual words are generally extended to the right, using a number of suffixes *(autóval, diszkóban, használhatjuk)*, while the Indo-European languages work backward from a word, or are left-tending *(an die See,* to the sea). Learning a synthetic, condensing structure seems to be more difficult than learning an analytic, divisive structure.

The truth is that Hungarian is different from the other European languages. This is only natural since the vast majority of the other European languages belong to the Indo-European family of languages. Hungarian belongs to the Finno-Ugrian family of languages. In many respects, it is an odd one even in that family. Even though the Hungarian language has been for several thousand years in an Indo-European environment, and even though a certain amount of Latinization (Indo-Europeanization) can be observed in it, it has maintained its individual characteristics in spite of the obvious interactions.

If someone who speaks an Indo-European language

wishes to become familiar with the non Indo-European Hungarian language, let him remember the magic sentence: "In the Hungarian language everything is reversed!" Teachers of Hungarian often say this as a form of encouragement. It obviously does not pertain to everything! There are always enough structural differences between the two languages to challenge the student.

Let us look at some examples in English and in Hungarian:

doboz - *om* - *ba* (→ tends to the right)
box   my   into

olvas - *tat* - *hat* - *ná* - *nak* (→ tends to the right)
read make(sy) could would they

But we will hear more about this in the coming chapters.

Hungarian Sounds and Letters

The Hungarian alphabet:

In Hungarian a separate letter is used to designate each sound. The only exceptions are the consonants *j* and *ly* which produce the identical *j* sound and are distinguished only in spelling. (*Ly* is an old *j* sound which is used only rarely in certain words and which causes considerable difficulties to Hungarian children, when they first learn to spell. *Jó* [good], and *lyuk* [hole] have the same sound today, and yet are spelled differently). There is no logical reason why the *j* sound in one word should be spelled *j* and in another *ly*. The two identical sounds remain in the Hungarian alphabet for purely traditional reasons.

The Hungarian vowels are: *a-á, e-é, i-í, o-ó, ö-ő, u-ú, ü-ű.* It can be seen that each vowel is paired. Those without an accent or with dots are short, those with accents or double accents are long. It is important to distinguish between the short and the long vowels, since the length of the vowel may affect the meaning of the word: *vad* (wild) - *vád* (accusation), *keres* (seek) - *kérés* (request), *tör* (break) - *tőr* (dagger).

The single Hungarian consonants are: *b, c, d, f, g, h, j, k, l, m, n, p, r, s, t, v, z.* These sounds exist in the Indo-European languages as well and only the sound value of *s, v* and *z* has to be learned. The groups consisting of two letters are a peculiarly Hungarian manifestation but represent a single sound. These are as follows: *cs, dz, dzs, gy, ly, ny, sz, ty,* and *zs.* These letter combination are usually confusing for the foreigner, who considers the double letters as though they were two sounds and tries to pronounce them accordingly. The *y* used as the second letter in the double letter combinations does not represent a separate vowel!

LETTER	HUNGARIAN NAME	LETTER	HUNGARIAN NAME
a	a	n	enn
á	á	ny	enny
b	bé	o	o, rövid o
c	cé	ó	ó, hosszú ó
cs	csé	ö	ö, rövid ö
d	dé	ő	ő, hosszú ő
dz	dzé	p	pé
dzs	dzsé	(q)	(kú)
e	e	r	err
é	é	s	ess
f	eff	sz	essz
g	gé	t	té
gy	gyé	ty	tyé
h	há	u	u, rövid u
i	i, rövid i	ú	ú, hosszú ú
í	í, hosszú í	ü	ü, rövid ü
j	jé	ű	ű, hosszú ű
k	ká	v	vé
l	ell	(w)	(dupla vé)
ly	ell-ipszilon-nal	(x)	(iksz)
		(y)	(ipszilon)
m	emm	z	zé
		zs	zsé

Figure 2. The Hungarian alphabet

31

There are seven cases where the student has to learn the sound created by the double letters. Whoever is aware of this should have no difficulty in pronouncing *Magyarország,* although for the uninitiated the *gy* and the *sz* have been known to produce problems. The same holds for the city of *Győr* or for the town of *Tihany,* on Lake Balaton.

The Hungarian language thus possesses $7+7=14$ vowels, 17 simple and 9 paired consonants, i.e., a total of 40 letters. *Dz, dzs* and *ty* appear in very few words and *ly* does not represent a separate sound. This reduces the total number of letters somewhat. There are letters which are common in other languages but occur only very rarely in Hungarian and are used primarily in foreign words: e.g.: *ch* (München, technika), *q* (quattrocento), *w* (Washington, watt), *x* (xerox, xilifon), and *y* (yard).

Hungarian typewriter and computer keyboards correspond precisely to international standards and the accented vowels are found at the edges of the keyboard.

In old Hungarian texts and in family names we find a number of antiquated forms of spelling: e.g: *eö=ö* - Eötvös Loránd (pronounced ötvös); *ch=cs,* e.g: Madách Imre (pronounced madács); *y=i* when it is used by itself, e.g.: Kölcsey Ferenc (pronounced kölcsei).

Adjacent consonants become assimilated and may fuse into a third sound.:

anya+-ja=anyja [annya] (his/her mother). The assimilation is indicated only in the pronunciation.

Budapest+-val/-vel= Budapest-tel (with Budapest). The assimilation is recognized in the written form as well.

lát+ja= látja [láttya] (he/she sees it). The assimilation is indicated only in the pronunciation.

In the Hungarian language, we tend to preserve the original spelling in personal names and frequently used words: Cervantes, Horatius, Shakespeare, cowboy, schilling, business, etc. Some words go over into the language and eventually will be spelled according to Hungarian usage. E.g., today we use *diszkó* for disco, *nejlon* for nylons, and *softver* for software.

The punctuation marks used in other languages are used in Hungarian in the same way. The most important ones are: "," *vessző* (comma), ":" *kettőspont* (colon), ";" *pontosvessző* (semicolon), "." *pont* (period), "!" *felkiáltójel* (exclamation point), "?" *kérdőjel* (question mark), and "..." *három pont* (triple period).

Vowel harmony:

Hungarian vowels are divided into two categories, front vowels: *e-é, ö-ő, ü-ű,* and back vowels: *a-á, o-ó, u-ú.* By and large, Hungarian word stems contain only vowels from one of these two sets – either front vowels or back vowels. Accordingly, we can distinguish "front words": *beszél* (he speaks), *kettő* (two), and "back words": *oroszlán* (lion), *három* (three). "Mixed words" include both front and back vowels: *leány* (girl), *virág* (flower).

One of the most important phonetic peculiarities of the Hungarian language (as in Finnish, Turkish and other Altaic languages) is vowel harmony, which means that most endings have two (or three) alternative forms differing only in the vowel. The selection of the correct form of the ending is determined by the vowel(s) of the word stem. In the Germanic languages the opposite is true: the suffix remains the same but the root word changes. E.g.: *rot - rötlich* (red - reddish), *rund - ründlich* (round - rounded).

Some endings with two forms are: *-ban/-ben, -nak/-nek, -tól/-től.* (Endings with two or three forms are indicated in grammatical descriptions by a hyphen and a slash.)

Some endings with three forms are: *-on/-en/-ön, -hoz/-hez/-höz, -kodik/-kedik/-ködik.*

Here are some examples to illustrate vowel harmony, i.e., the harmony between the vowels of the word stem and those of the ending(s):

33

Front words: **front   front   front**
           beszél   -get   -nek   (They are chatting.)
           stem   endings
Others: *vér-ben* (in blood), *egyszerű-ség* (simplicity), *énekel-nek* (they are singing).

Back words: **back   back   back**
           oroszlán -ok   -tól   (from the lions)
           stem   endings
Others: *harmat-ban* (in dew), *barát-ság* (friendship), *autó-nak* (for a/the car).

Mixed words usually get the back variant of the endings:
           mixed   back   back
           leány   -ok   -hoz   (to the girls)
           stem   endings
Others: *biká-nak* (for a bull), *szigorú-ság* (severity), *kíván-nak* (they wish, crave).

The three-form endings make it possible to achieve perfect harmony even in terms of lip-position: these suffixes have three alternative forms, one with the back vowel *o,* another with the front unrounded *e,* and a third with the front rounded *ö.*

Back words: *ág-on* (on the branch), *asztal-hoz* (to the table), *mosa-kodik* (he washes himself).

Front, unrounded words: *ég-en* (in the sky), *kert-hez* (to the garden), *vendéges-kedik* (he entertains guests).

Front words in the final syllable with rounded front vowels: *(ö-ő, ü-ű):* *föld-ön* (on the ground), *erdő-höz* (to the forest), *fésül-ködik* (he combs his hair).

Those learning Hungarian often use the wrong endings. Thus: *föld-en* (correctly: *föld-ön*). Naturally, even the incorrect use will be comprehensible just like when someone uses German pronouns incorrectly. It may serve as some comfort to the learner that there are some Hungarian words which are used in two different ways even by Hungarian speakers: *Ágnesnek - Ágnesnak* (for Ágnes), *hotelben - hotelban* (in the hotel), *parkettje - parkettja* (its flooring).

Word divisions – front and back pairs:

Several languages, including Hungarian, use the front and back phonetic structures in forming words. By changing the base tone, a front word is given a back pair and vice versa. We call this word divisions when a word splits in its meaning and becomes two separate and different words. Yet the specific meaning or general meaning of the pair of words remains related. Their phonetic form suggests a difference in intensity or degree. The front forms suggest nearness, smallness and plurality, the back forms suggest distance, largeness and greater intensity:

itt	*ott*	here - there
emez	*amaz*	this - that
ekkor	*akkor*	now - then
kever	*kavar*	mix - stir
gömböc	*gombóc*	roly-poly - dumpling
gyűr	*gyúr*	wrinkle - knead
köröm	*karom*	nail - talon
cseléd	*család*	servant - family
bőg	*búg*	cry - hum
libeg	*lobog*	dangle - wave
töröl	*tarol*	wipe - glean

Similar phenomena may be seen in Indo-European languages as well (e.g.: the German *hier - dort* – here - there).

Large word families:

In the Hungarian language there are a number of word families which are characterized by a narrow kinship in form and meaning. The similarities in form rest on the sameness of the consonants (or on their regular relationship), and on having at least one common element of meaning. One of the basic forms is: CVC or consonant-vowel-consonant (i.e., one changeable vowel between two consonants):

> P + vowel + R (related to fire, burning,
>   inflammation, etc.)
> *PAR-ázs* (embers)
> *PÁR-ol* (braise)
> *PER -gel* (caramelize), *-zsel* (sear), *-nye*
>   (flying ashes)
> *PIR-ít* (roast)
> *POR-ít* (turn into dust)
> *PÖR-köl* (singe)

> P + vowel + R (related to circles and
>   circling, rotating)
> *PAR-ittya* (slingshot)
> *PÁR-ta* (ribbon, ring)
> *POR-tya* (a tour - round trip)
> *PÖR-ög, -dül* (rotate)

In spite of their similar form and related meanings, the above words are considered etymologically to be derived from several languages and are probably mostly loanwords.

Another large word family that has been the subject of several studies is: K + vowel + R, e.g.: *kar-, ker-, kör-* and *kür-*. There are two different kinships between these words:

1. animal chasing and herding words (e.g., *kur-rogat, kur-jongat, haj-kur-ál, ker-get, kür, be-kür,* etc. – these all relate to chasing, herding or corralling animals);

2. words meaning roundness or circularity (e.g. *kar-ika, ker-ek, ker-ék, ker-ít, kör-ít, kor-lát, kör-ös, kör-öz*).

Naturally, not all linguists believe that there is a kinship between all these words, but the phenomenon does bear a peculiar linguistic trait.

Diminutives – primarily with suffixes:

In some words, changing the second stem vowel to *i* produces a diminutive effect:

kapar ≈ *kapargál* ≈ *kapirgál* (scratches ≈ scratches the surface)
farag ≈ *faragcsál* ≈ *farigcsál* (carves ≈ whittles).

The *i* sound generally seems to be the sound of smallness (vivacity, cheerfulness and youthful feelings): *viháncol* (giggle), *vigyorog* (grin), *vidám* (cheerful), *víg* (lively), *sír* (cry), *pityereg* (sob), *csibe* (chick), *csicsereg* (twitter), *pirinyó* (tiny), *csipog* (chirp).

In Hungarian there are numerous opportunities for the dimination of nouns and names. The most common form is the addition of a diminutive suffix to make the new word be smaller or more personal than the stem word. The language of the fairy tales, baby talk and love talk contains many diminutive terms. In the Hungarian language, there are at least 100 diminutive suffixes:

-cska, -cske: láb-acska (little foot), *felhő-cske* (little cloud)
-ka, -ke: asztal-ka (little table), *Jós-ka* (little Joseph), *Feri-ke* (little Francis)
-i: Ág-i (little Agnes), *Fer-i* (little Francis)
-csi: Jan-csi (little John), *fron-csi* (a diminutive for Forint
-ca: Te-ca (little Theresa)
-ci: An-ci (little Anna), *Ber-ci* (little Bartholomew)
-u: ap-u (Daddy), *any-u* (Mummy)
-us: Ann-us (little Anna), *ap-us* (daddy), *cic-us* (kitten)

-ica: Kat-ica (little Kathleen)
-uci: Any-uci (little mother)
-ikó: ház-ikó (little house), *lád-ikó* (little box)
-csa, -cse: Bor-csa (little Barbara), *tó-csa* (little puddle),
    üveg-cse (little glass)

Reduplication – coordinating word combinations:
Reduplication seems to be a phenomenon related to the phonetic diminutive formation. Reduplication, in this context, means the repetition of a word in a slightly different form. In some reduplications, the consonants are the same and the vowels change:

dirmeg-dörmög	(mutter)
csireg-csörög	(rattle)
lim-lom	(trash)
ripsz-ropsz	(tearing sound)
tik-tak	(tic-toc)

In other cases, the vowels remain the same and the consonants change or may be added to the front of the first word:

ámul-bámul	(wonder)
illeg-billeg	(waver)
elegy-belegy	(medley)
apa-papa	(father)
csiga-biga	(snail)
Andi-Bandi	(Andy)
cica-mica	(kitty-cat)

Both vowel and consonant may change:

bikk-makk	(acorn)
oké-okszi	(O.K.)

Reduplications occur in other languages as well, but in the Hungarian language they prosper, are common in everyday usage, and new forms are constantly cropping up. These reduplications are generally juvenile or slang forms where one of the pair (occasionally both) are real words while the duplication-word is simply a phonetic echo. Such reduplications are used as forms of endearment, or to emphasize something, or to tease.

The metaphysics of phonetics:

While sounds, as such, have no meaning as far as we know, they still seem to affect meaning. This was the subject of experimentation. Hungarian speakers have given a striking answer to questions dealing with the "meaning" of certain sounds.

Question:	%
Which is smaller, *i* or *u*?	88 to 12
Which is sadder, *i* or *u*?	8 to 92
Which is wilder, r or *l* ?	99 to 1
Which is sharper, *s* or *sz*?	33 to 67

The musicality of the Hungarian language:

Tourists unfamiliar with the language of a given country judge it frequently on the basis of its resonance, melody and the average intensity with which it is spoken. Many have studied the esthetics of sounds. Statistical tables have been prepared about the weight (frequency) of certain individual sounds. Simplified statistics of sounds indicate the proportion of vowels and consonants in a language. If we accept the principle that the musicality and beauty of a language is a function of the ratio of these two factors, then a rank ordering can be accomplished of the harsher and softer sounding languages. On this basis, Hungarian is among the more musical languages:

	Vowel	Consonant
Finnish	51	49
Italian	48	52
Ancient Greek	46	54
Spanish	45	55
Gaelic	45	55
Latin	44	56
Ottoman-Turkish	43	57
French	41	59
Hungarian	41	59
Tatar	41	59
German	36	64
Czech	35	65

The Hungarian language prefers the more open sounds and thus to make it understandable and clear, it has to be carefully articulated (the mouth has to be opened wider). In other languages a more closed articulation is typical.

Onomatopoeia:
There is a large number of onomatopoetic words in the Hungarian language. In their phonetic content, the onomatopoetic words imitate or suggest the original sound or meaning. They may be natural, environmental sounds: *susog* (rustle), *puffan* (thump), *durr* (bang), *csörög* (rattle). Animal sounds: *cincog* (squeak), *nyávog* (miaow), *kotkodácsol* (cluck), *kukurékol* (crow), *vau-vau* (bow-vow). Man-made sounds: *krákog* (hawk), *köhög* (cough), *sóhajt* (sigh). Animal names: *kakukk* (cuckoo), *pitypalatty* (quail), *cica* (kitty). Baby talk sounds: *csecse*, *bibi*, *baba*, *mama*. Playful, imitative sounds: *pszi* (spray), *sihuhu* (train), *ni-no* (police siren).

The Hungarian language is particularly rich in naming animal sounds. Among the verbs relative to the phonation of birds, there are many onomatopoetic words:

fülemüle (nightingale)	*csattog*
szarka (magpie)	*cserreg*
veréb (sparrow)	*csipog*
rigó (oriole)	*fütyöl, füttyeget*
bagoly (owl)	*huhog, rikolt, sí, üvölt*
gerle (dove)	*kacag, turbékol, nyög, búg*
gólya (stork)	*kelepel, kerepel*

Palindromes:

A number of people have drawn attention to the fact that in the Hungarian language there are a large number of palindromic words, e.g., *bab* (bean), *búb* (crown of the head), *csecs* (breast), *csöcs* (tit), *gőg* (pride), *púp* (hump), *apa* (father), *anya* (mother), *ara* (bride), *eke* (plow), *ürü* (ram), *jaj* (ouch), *sas* (eagle), *zúz* (bruise), *tát* (open), *tét* (stake), *vív* (fence). There are longer words as well, which are not roots: *inni* (to drink), *előle* (ahead of him), *darab* (piece), *görög*, (Greek) *kerek* (round), *konok* (obstinate), *közök* (intervals), *körök* (circles), *legel* (grazes), *lehel* (he pants), *lohol* (he hurries), *lepel* (shroud), *magam* (myself), *mosom* (I wash it), *rájár* (he deserves it), *sebes* (wounded), *soros* (due to), *saras* (muddy), *sörös* (beery), *tehet* (he may), *temet* (he buries), *teret* (the place).

It is an old popular pass-time to make palindromic sentences. They read and mean the same from both directions:

A bátya gatyába	(the brother in underpants)
Adósom a mosoda	(The laundry owes me)
Géza, kék az ég	(Géza, the sky is blue)
Indul a görög aludni	(The Greek is going to sleep)
Indul a kutya, a tyúk aludni	(The dog, the hen are going to sleep)
Ír a Mari	(Mari writes)
Kár a papnak rák	(Crab is wasted on the priest)

Hungarian Words and Sentences

The structure of Hungarian words:
The characteristic format for Hungarian words is as follows:

Prefixes	Roots	Endings/Suffixes
el -	*megy* -	*ünk* (we depart)
away	go	we
leg -	*nagy* -	*obb-ak-é-i* (belonging to the largest ones)
superlative	large	belonging to them
	ház -	*as-ok-nak* (for the married ones)
	house	married-plural-for

The prefix may be a verbal prefix attached to the front of the verb: *el-megy* (he goes away), *oda-néz* (he looks there, he looks at [something]), or it may be a sign of superlative adjective: *leg-nagyobb* (the largest).

As to the endings, their number is very large, and their importance in the Hungarian language is overwhelming: Hungarian is an agglutinative language.

Preposition vs. Endings:
In general, the Indo-European languages express grammatical relationships with prepositions. In Hungarian there are no prepositions: *a hegyekben* (in the mountains), *a hegységekben* (in the mountain ranges), *társamhoz* (to my

companion), *társaságomhoz* (to my company), *társaságom-ban* (in my company), *az asztal alatt* (under the table).

(In exceptional situations a postposition may move ahead of the word, and, in fact, become a "preposition": *a városon át - át a városon* [across the city], *a Dunán túl - túl a Dunán* [beyond the Danube], *Budapesten kívül - kívül Budapesten* [outside Budapest].)

The grammar of Hungarian as a native language divides endings into three categories:

1. derivational suffixes *(képzők)* - word-building endings which create new words, often changing the part-of-speech category as well:

ház-as-ság-i   (house, married, marriage, marriage)
                noun adjective noun adjective
kert-ész-kedik   (garden, gardener, does some gardening)
                noun   noun   verb

2. signs *(jelek)* - change words to a lesser degree (than derivational suffixes) and generally mark quantity, possession, time or mood:

virág-ok, virág-é, olvasott volna (flowers, something of a flower, he would have read something)

3. inflectional suffixes *(ragok)* - sentence-building endings, which in the case of verbs denote numbers and persons and in the case of nouns denote adverbial conditions:

megy - megy-ünk, ház - ház-ban (he goes - we go, house - in the house)

Endings have a characteristic sequence in Hungarian:
- derivational suffixes are the "innermost" elements, closest to the root of the word:

ház-as-ság   (house - married - marriage);

- signs are intermediate elements: *házasság-ok* (marriages);

- inflectional suffixes are always the final, terminal elements:

házasságok-ban (in marriages)

The grammar of Hungarian as a foreign language is a bit different: it does not usually differentiate between the above mentioned three categories. From the foreign speaker's point of view, it does not really matter what labels the many endings in Hungarian have. From the learner's viewpoint, what matters is that he be able to recognize and use the endings properly.

Endings:

Verbs may have a tense-sign (past and future sign, since the most frequently used present tense has no sign), mood indicators (conditional and imperative signs, since the most frequently used declarative mood has no sign).

There are two primary conjugations (with definite and indefinite object), and two incomplete, limited conjugations (the so-called *"ikes"* one, using **-ik** as a personal suffix and formerly passive, and the one using **-lak/-lek,** indicating a definite object in the second person). In certain situations the Hungarian language uses an auxiliary term to indicate tense and mood relationships instead of a suffix and in this it resembles the Indo-European languages, e.g.: *menni fogok* (I will go), and *örültem volna* (I would have been pleased).

Tense:

vár (wait) - *kér* (asks for) present – present tense has no sign

vár-t (waited) - *kér-t* (asked for) – **-t/-tt** past tense sign

várni fog (will wait) - *kérni fog* (will ask for) – the conjugatable **fog** is an auxiliary verb and the sign for the future tense

Mood:

vár (wait) - *kér* (asks for) - the declarative mood
has no sign

vár-na (would wait) - *kér-ne* (would ask) -
the conditional mood has *-na/-ne* as its sign

vár-j (wait!) - *kér-j* (ask for somethin) -
the imperative mood has *-j* and a variety of other signs

Indefinite conjugation:

várok, vársz, vár, várunk, vártok, várnak (I wait, you
wait, etc.) – declarative mood present tense

"Ikes" conjugation (*-ik* personal suffix, formerly passive): *eszem, eszel, eszik* (I eat, you eat, he eats) –
declarative mood, present tense

Definite conjugation: *várom, várod, várja, várjuk, várjátok, várják* (I wait, you wait, etc. for a specific something, e.g.: the train) – declarative mood, present tense

-lak, -lek conjugation: *vár-lak* (I wait for you)
declarative mood, present tense

Nouns can have approximately 20 case endings,
depending on one's linguistic orientation. (Some say 17,
since the possessive and dative case endings are the same.)
The number of case endings is another peculiarity of the
Hungarian language, since, e.g., German has only 4, Latin
5, and Russian 6. In the Indo-European languages there
are only traces of case endings, while the Hungarian language has a well-developed system of cases:

1. *ház* (house) - no suffix (nominative): *Épül a ház.*
(The house is being built.)

2. *ház-at* - objective case (accusative): *Látom a házat.* (I see the house.)

3. *ház-nak* - possessive case (genitive): *Betört a háznak az ablaka.* (The window of the house was broken.)

In Hungarian, the dative case is the same as the genitive: See #14.

4. *ház-ban* (in the house): Answers the question: where? indicating an internal locational determinant (inessive). *Ebben a házban lakom.* (I live in this house.)

5. *ház-ba* (into the house). Answers the question: whereto? indicating an internal locational determinant (illative). *Megyek a házba.* (I go into the house.)

6. *ház-ból* (from the house). Answers the question: wherefrom? indicating an internal locational determinant (elative). *A házból elköltöztek.* (They moved from the house.)

7. *ház-on* (on the house). Answers the question: where? indicating an external locational determinant (superessive). *A házon van egy gólyafészek.* (There is a stork's nest on the house.)

8. *ház-ról* (from the house). Answers the question: from where? indicating an external locational determinant (delative). *A házról hullik a vakolat.* (The plaster is falling from the house.)

9. *ház-ra* (on to the house). Answers the question: whereto? indicating an external locational determinant (sublative). *A házra kitűzték a lobogót.* (They hoisted the flag onto the house.)

10. *ház-nál* (by the house). Answers the question: where? indicating an external locational determinant (adessive). *Annál a háznál álljon meg!* (Stop at that house.)

11. *ház-tól* (from the house). Answers the question:

wherefrom? indicating an external locational determinant (ablative). *Elköltözött a háztól.* (He moved away from the house.)

12. *ház-hoz* (to the house). Answers the question: whereto? indicating an external locational determinant (allative). *Az utast házhoz viszi a taxi.* (The cab takes the passenger to the house.)

13. *ház-ig* (until the house). Answers the question: how far? indicating an external locational or temporal determinant (terminative). *Egészen a házig futott.* (He ran all the way to the house). *Halálig hű maradt.* (He stayed faithful until death.)

14. *ház-nak* (for the house) (dative). *A háznak erős alapot építettek.* They built (for) the house a strong foundation.

15. *ház-ként* (as a house). Conditional determinant (formalis). *Az ősember számára a barlangok szolgáltak házként.* (For pre-historic man, a cave served as a house.)

16. *ház-zá* (into a house) (translative). *A romépület szép házzá alakult.* (The ruin was turned into a nice house.)

17. *ház-zal* (with a house) (associative - instrumental). *A házzal kertet is vettek.* (They bought a garden with the house.)

18. *ház-ért* (for the house). Causal and terminal determinant (causalis-finalis). *Sokat dolgozott ezért a házért.* (He worked hard for this house.)

Nouns and verbs form a separate paradigm:

a) *kapok, kapsz, kap, kapunk, kaptok, kapnak* (I get, you get, etc.) (indefinite conjugation)

b) *kapom, kapod, kapja, kapjuk, kapjátok, kapják* (I get it, you get it, etc.) (definite conjugation)

c) *napom, napod, napja, napunk, napotok, napjuk* (my day, your day, etc.) (possessive declination for one object)

d) *napjaim, napjaid, napjai, napjaink, napjaitok, napjaik* (my days, your days, etc.) (possessive declination with more than one object)

Kapjuk (verb) and *napjuk* (noun) are very similar to each other for historical reasons, but cause no problem whatever in communication.

Verb conjugations – definite and indefinite:

In Hungarian, different verb forms are used depending on whether the verb has a direct object and whether the object of the verb is definite or not. There is no such distinction in English.

Látok egy házat. (indefinite)	I see a house.
Látom a házat. (definite)	I see the house.

Verbs, then, have two conjugations, i.e., two sets of endings, definite and indefinite. This fascinating feature of the Hungarian language can cause complications at times, although the basic principles are comprehensible. Let us see some examples.

Objects are definite (and then stand with a definite verb form) when they:

– have a definite article:
Látom a házat.   I see **the** house.

– have possessive markers:
Látom a házadat.   I see **your** house.
Látom a háznak a tetejét.   I see **the** roof **of** the house.

– have a demonstrative pronoun:
Látom azt a házat.   I see **that** house.

48

– are expressed with a clause identifying the object:

| *Látom, **ami az*** | I see **what** |
| *elmúlt években épült.* | **was built in the past years.** |

– are expressed with a third person pronoun, whether stated or unstated:

*Látom (**őt, őket, azt**).* I see (**him/her, them, that, those**).

– are expressed with an "*-ik*" ending pronoun:

| ***Melyiket** látom?* | **Which one** do I see? |
| *Az **egyik** házat látom.* | I see **one** of the houses. |

– are proper nouns:

*Látom **Katit.*** I see **Kati.**

Objects are indefinite (and then stand with an indefinite verb form) when they:

– have no articles:

Házakat látok. I see houses.

– have indefinite articles:

***Egy** házat látok.* I see **a** house.

– have number structures:

***Öt/Sok** házat látok.* I see **five/many** houses.

– are expressed with pronouns other than the "*-ik*" group:

***Mit** látok?*	**What** do I see?
***Hány** házat látok?*	**How many** *houses do I see?*
***Milyen** házat látok?*	**What sort** of house/houses do I see?

– are expressed with first and second person pronouns, whether stated or unstated:

| *Látlak (**téged**).* | I see (**you**). |
| *Péter lát (**engem**).* | Péter sees (**me**). |

Of course, the indefinite conjugation is used when the verb is intransitive, i.e., it does not and cannot have an object:

Minden reggel futok.	I run/jog every morning.
Hol alszol?	Where do you sleep?

Word formation: derivation:

Numerous suffixes may be added to verbs and to nouns and in this way new words or new meanings may be created. There are four ways of doing this:

1. Verbs from verbs:

Suffixes indicating repetitive activity - frequentative suffixes. (According to some calculations, there are 46 different frequentative suffixes in the Hungarian language!):

-gat/-get: *néz-eget* (he keeps looking), *törül-get* (he keeps wiping)

-ong/-eng/-öng: *tol-ong* (he keeps crowding), *zsib-ong* (it keeps aching)

-oz/-ez/-öz: *kiált-oz(ik)* (He keeps yelling), *sóhajt-oz(ik)* (he keeps sighing), *önt-öz* (he keeps watering), *köt-öz* (he keeps binding)

Suffixes indicating instantaneous activity (motion). According to calculations, there are 36, e.g.: *-an/-en: durr-an* (he explodes), *csobb-an* (he splashes); *-ant/ent: dobb-ant* (he throbs), *tüssz-ent* (he sneezes); *-int: köh-int* (he coughs), *csavar-int* (he gives it a turn).

Reflexive suffixes: *-ódik/-ődik: húz-ódik* (he withdraws himself), *ver-ődik* (he smashes himself), *-kodik/-kedik/-ködik: mos-akodik* (he washes himself), *fésül-ködik* (he combs himself) *ver-ekedik* (he exchanges blows).

Factitive or causative suffix - making somebody else do

something: **-at/-et, -tat/-tet:** *olvas-tat* (make somebody read), *néz-et* (make somebody look), *vág-tat* (he gallops).

Passive suffixes: **-atik/-etik, -tatik/-tetik:** *ad-atik* (it is given), *vét-etik* (it is being purchased).

Potential suffixes which allow something to happen: -**hat/-het:** *dolgoz-hat* (he may work), *ír-hat* (he may write).

2. Making verbs from nouns: *bor – bor-oz* (wine - drinks wine).

3. Making nouns from verbs: *fut – fut-ás* (he runs - flight).

4. Making nouns from nouns: *király-né* (king-queen), *Nagy Zoltán-né* (Mrs. Zoltán Nagy), *só-tlan* (salt-free), *szó-tlan* (word-less, mute).

It is most interesting that several endings with different functions can be attached to a single verb or noun. Thus, a number of functions may be condensed into a single word form: *lát* (he sees), *lát-juk* (we see it), *lát-hat-juk* (we can see it).

In Hungarian, a single word form - actually a complete sentence - e.g.: *néz-előd-het-né-k,* can express what in English would take several: I could look around (if I wished).

The aggregation of endings leads to the formation of a number of different expressions in Hungarian. Quite long "word-snakes" can be created, e.g.: *meghívhatnálak* (I could invite you), *hiteltelenségemet* (as to my absence of credit), *állhatatlanságotokat* (your lack of reliability). Children frequently make up perfectly correct, extremely long words, which would ordinarily not be used: *Ezt a káposztástálat teljesen elkáposztástalanítottátok* (You have made this plate of sour-crout completely sour-crout free).

51

Simple verb tense system:

Today the Hungarian system of verb tenses is simpler than that of the Indo-European languages. The Hungarian language today has a single present, past and future tense:

Present: *olvad* (it melts), *néz* (he looks)

Past: *olvadt* (it melted), *néz-ett* (he looked)

Future: *olvadni fog* (it will melt), *nézni fog* (he will look)

Until the beginning of the 20th century, Hungarian literature still retained remnants of a more complete system of tenses and there were antiquated single and composite pasts and futures. Early Hungarian clearly had a richer system of tenses, although their presence may have been partially due to the influence of Latin which was the language of the learned classes. Traces of the antiquated forms can still be found in some of the more isolated dialects. Contemporary Hungarian writers, (Péter Esterházy, Péter Nádas and Ferenc Temesi) occasionally use these old forms for stylistic purposes: *írtam vala* - I had (once) written, *olvasám* - I was reading (continuous).

Participles:

The number of participles is greater and their role is more important in Hungarian than in the Indo-European languages. In the dictionaries, the Hungarian verb appears in the third person, singular, which is considered to be the principal form of the verb. The infinitive, used in other languages, reveals practically nothing about the characteristics of the verb in the Hungarian language. The infinitive does have a characteristic feature, however. It can be conjugated. This is not the case for the infinitives in the Indo-European languages: *fut - fut-ni: fut-n-om, fut-n-od, fut-n-ia, fut-n-unk, fut-n-otok, fut-n-iuk (kell)* (he runs - to run: I [have to] run, you [have to] run, etc.). *Ma is kell futnunk.* (We have to run today also.)

There are three forms of the participle:

Present (ongoing): *-ó/-ő* olvas-*ó* (reader), *néz-ő* (looker)

Past (completed): *-t/-tt* olvas-*ott* (read), *néz-ett* (looked)

Future (to be done): ***-andó/-endő*** olvas-*andó* (to be read), *néz-endő* (to be looked at)

The adverbial participle (adverbum verbale): ***-va/-ve, -ván/-vén*** *fut-va* (running), *nyit-va* (open), *fut-ván* (having run). *Az üzlet nyitva van* (The store is open). *Futva érkezett* (He came running).

Passive construction:

Passive construction is only fragmentary in the Hungarian language. There is a suffix to make a passive verb *(-atik/-etik, -tatik/-tetik)*, which can even be conjugated but it is used only very rarely: *A levél postára ad-atik* (The letter is being put into the mail). Instead, we would say: *Postára adjuk a levelet* (We mail the letter), or: *Postára adják* (They mail the letter).

Adverbial infinitives may have a passive meaning: *Az üzlet zárva van* (The store is closed).

Signs indicating gender:

Hungarian nouns have no gender, but the Hungarian language does make certain distinctions in some words denoting an occupation. Words referring specifically to females: *kézilány* (handmaiden), *eladólány* (sales-lady), *óvónő* (female kindergarten teacher), *ápolónő* (female nurse).

Exceptionally, these may have a male counterpart: *óvóbácsi* (male kindergarden teacher), *ápolóférfi* (male nurse), or a word may have an exclusively male connotation: *házibarát* (lover, literally: house friend).

Words having a form for each gender include:

medikus - medika	(male medical student- female medical student)
komikus - komika	(comedian - comedienne)
doktor - doktornő	(doctor - lady doctor)

Words which may indicate either gender but in which the female gender may be emphasized are:

elnök - elnöknő	(president)
	(*nő* means woman)
tanár - tanárnő	(teacher)
művész - művésznő	(artist)
színész - színésznő	(actor - actress)
bemondó - bemondónő	(announcer)
újságíró - újságírónő	(journalist)
szerkesztő - szerkesztőnő	(editor)

Since the political changes in 1989, there has been considerable confusion in the form of address to both men and women. The pre-war *úr - úrnő, úrasszony, kisasszony,* (mister, madam, lady, miss) were replaced under socialism, particularly under official or formal circumstances, by *elvtárs - elvtársnő* (comrade). After the change in regime, the address to men was immediately re-established as *úr* (mister). It is true, however, that even under socialism most people still said *tanár úr* (mister teacher), *doktor úr* (mister doctor), and not comrade. Address to women is still in a confused state:

úrnő seems archaic, peculiar and aristocratic,

úrasszony is also old-fashioned and too fancy.

Children use *néni* (aunt) very frequently even to women not related to them.

In general, women are addressed with *asszonyom* (literally: my woman), *hölgyem* (my lady), *kisasszony* (literally: little woman), or an address is carefully avoided.

54

Expressing location and direction – "Tri-directionalism":

Space suffixes in Hungarian can be perceived as belonging to three sets:

– one indicating movement towards a position (Where to?, "Whither?" - *Hová?*),

– one indicating a state of rest (Where? - *Hol?*), and

– one indicating movement away from the position (Where from? "Whence?" - *Honnan?*)

Based on Jerry Payne's interpretation, nouns can also be perceived as belonging to three basic types:

– one associated with closed spaces (shops, houses, schools, boxes, etc.),

– one associated with flat surfaces (tables, city squares, the ground, etc.), and

– one associated with points in space (trees, monuments, faraway destinations, human beings, etc.).

Accordingly, place suffixes can be grouped as follows:

	Where to?	**Where?**	**Where from?**
"house"	házba	házban	házból
"room"	terembe	teremben	teremből
"table"	asztalra	asztalon	asztalról
"ground"	földre	földön	földről
"tree"	fához	fánál	fától
„Erzsi"(name)	Erzsihez	Erzsinél	Erzsitől

The fact that a noun tends to belong to one group does not exclude other variations: we normally go *into* the house *(házba)*; a little bird, however, is usually sitting *on* the house (*házon* - flat surface ending); and when leaving for a long time, we might wave good-bye to our house (*búcsúzik a háztól* - point in space ending). Other languages may have similar lists of place endings, but rarely do they get so systematic and structured as they are in Hungarian.

Postpositions indicating location and direction often have three forms as well:

alá, alatt, alól	to+below, below, from+below
elé, előtt, elől	to+in front of, in front of, from+in front of
mellé, mellett,mellől	to+next to, next to, from+next to

Articles:

The Hungarian article indicates whether the following noun is definite or indefinite. The definite article has two forms: *a,* when the noun begins with a consonant, and *az* when the noun begins with a vowel: *a Duna* (the Danube), *az asztal* (the table).

The indefinite article is: ***egy: egy asztal*** (a table).

The use of articles in English and in Hungarian have very little in common:

Horses are animals, but: *A ló állat.*

Life is hard, but: *Az élet nehéz.*

Possessive construction:

In the Hungarian language the possessive construction is precisely the reverse from the usual Indo-European form. In general the possessor precedes the possessed: *a szülők háza* (the parents' house); *a kert virág-a* (the flower of the garden). The possessor either has no suffix or we may use the ***-nak/-nek*** dative case. The possessed receives the possessive/personal suffix. In rare instances – quite correctly – the sequence may be reversed and will now conform to the pattern of the Indo-European languages. In this instance, the genitive possessive suffix must be included: *ház-a a szülők-nek* (the house of the parents).

The phenomenon of the subjective genitive and of the objective genitive is interesting in that thus the possessive construction may mean two different things. This phenomenon exists in the reversed Hungarian construction just as it does in other languages:

az apa szeretete (the love of the father) can mean:
a) the father loves
b) the father is being loved

The uninflected attribute:

The Hungarian language uses pronouns, participles and numerals without any suffixes when attached to a noun, and no attempt is made to adjust them according to the form assumed by the noun: *jó ember* (a good man), *jó embereket* (good men). If the attribute is placed after the noun, then it must be reconciled with the form of the noun: *Napóleon, a legyőzött* (Napoleon the defeated), *Napóleont, a legyőzöttet* (the defeated Napoleon).

Numeric constructions:

It is a peculiarity of the Hungarian language that it does not reconcile in a numeric construction. The noun following the number is always in the singular regardless of the number: *egy ember* (one man), *tíz ember* (ten men). This is true in all aspects of the language. Thus: *száz forint* (100 forints), *két liter bor* (two liters of wine), *három tucat rózsa* (three dozen roses).

A sentence without a verb and a sentence consisting only of a verb:

The Hungarian verb differs from the verbs of the Indo-European languages. In Hungarian it is possible to have a complete sentence without a verb: *Pista katona* (Pista is a soldier), *Elizabeth királynő* (Elizabeth is queen), *Szomorú a szeme* (his eyes are sad). In these cases the substantive verb may be omitted. The same sentences, if referring to the past or to the future, must include the substantive verb: *Pista katona volt* (Pista was a soldier), *Pista katona lesz* (Pista will be a soldier), *Szomorú volt a szeme* (his eyes were sad).

There are also sentences which consist of a single verb. *Jöttem* (I came), *láttam* (I saw it), *győztem* (I conquered). What makes this possible is that in Hungarian the personal suffix on the verb indicates the subject (I), and also indicates the object and the time.

The "to have" ("got") constructions:

Hungarian expresses the idea of possession not through a verb, as in English (I *have* a house, etc.), German, Latin or French, but by using a construction involving the possessed forms and the verb *van* (there is) or *nincs* (there is not):

*Nekem **van** házam.*	I have (got) a house.
*Nekem **nincs** házam.*	I do not have a house.
	I haven't got a house.

Verbal prefixes:

Verbal prefixes are probably the most interesting and characteristic elements of the Hungarian language and they form a specific verbal prefix system. Verbal prefixes, attached firmly to the front end of the verb are known in several languages. In Russian and Latin they can never be separated from the verb. In German, there are separable and fixed verbal prefixes.

The verbal prefix creates a new word or gives the old word a new meaning.

The number of Hungarian verbal prefixes is very large and growing, since the living language can endow a number of adverbs with verbal prefix functions. A few frequently used verbal prefixes follow. Where a direct translation is not meaningful, an example is given: *abba- (abbahagy* - stop doing), *alá-* (under), *át-* (across), *be-* (into), *bele-* (into), *egybe-* (into one), *el-* (away), *ellen-* (against), *elő-* (forward), *előre-* (to the front), *fel-/föl-* (up), *fenn-/fönn-* (on top), *hátra-* (back), *haza-* (homeward), *hozzá-* (to), *ide-* (hither), *keresztül-* (across), *ketté-* (in half), *ki-* (out), *körül-* (around), *közbe-* (in between), *közre-* (surround), *külön-* (separate), *le-* (down), *meg- (meg-eszik* - he eats it up), *mellé-* (alongside), *neki-* (up against), *oda-* (thereto), *össze-* (together), *rá-* (onto), *rajta-* (on top), *széjjel-* (apart), *szembe-* (facing), *szerte-* (scatter), *szét-* (apart), *tele-* (full), *tova-* (away), *tönkre-* (ruin), *túl-* (beyond), *ujjá-* (anew), *újra-* (again), *utána-* (after), *végbe-* (terminally), *végig-* (all the way), *vissza-* (back), etc.

Almost every Hungarian verbal prefix may be separated from its verb, and in a variety of ways:

a) The verbal prefix is before the verb, firmly attached to it, written as a single word: *elmegy* (leaves), *meglát* (sees, catches sight of).

b) The verbal prefix is after the verb and is written as a separate word: *megy el* (leaves), *lát meg* (sees, catches sight of).

c) Other words, usually auxiliary words, may be interposed between the verbal prefix and the verb: *el nem megyek* (I am not leaving), *el tudok menni* (I can leave), *ment végre el* (left at last).

Another peculiarity of the Hungarian verbal prefixes is that they may be reduplicated. These express repetitiveness, e.g., *ki-ki néz* (he keeps looking out). The juxtaposition of verbal prefixes with different meanings is suitable to express more complicated events: *föl-le jár* (he goes/paces up and down), *oda-vissza megy* (he goes back and forth).

Inflected suffixes:

Some suffixes may appear all by themselves and these can be inflected further. These will form the so-called personally inflected adverbs (case ending forms + personal possessive endings): *-val,-vel*: *vel-em, vel-ed, vel-e, vel-ünk, vel-etek, vel-ük* (with me, with you, with him, etc.). For the purposes of emphasis, even the personal pronoun may be attached to them: *én-vel-em, te-vel-ed* (with me, with you, etc.).

A similar term in Finnish is *minulta, sinulta* and the Spanish *conmigo* = *velem-vel* (with me - with). In Latin we may see the reverse: *mecum, tecum secum* (me with, you with, he with). In Gaelic there are forms which are hauntingly similar to the Hungarian personally inflected adverbs. E.g.: *fo* (under), *fodham* (under me), *fodhad* (under you), *fodha* (under him); *ann* (within), *annam* (within me), *annad* (within you), *anna* (within him). There are similar findings in the Irish tongue. Thus, while this system is the richest and most widely used in Hungarian, it is not a unique characteristic.

Word order:

According to the universal rules of syntax, the three principal elements of a sentence are the subject (S), the object (O), and the verb (V). Logically these can be arranged in six ways (three ways in declaratory sentences). The majority of the Uralian languages are of the SOV type, while Finnish is of the SVO type, and this latter type is also characteristic of Hungarian. SVO = *Apám vett egy házat* (My father bought a house). In English the SVO sequence is mandatory.

Emphasis (focus):

In the Hungarian language, the word order is intimately linked to the focus of the sentence. If the word to be emphasized is the verb, it is generally placed at the beginning of the sentence:

Megölte a királyt tegnap este egy bérgyilkos (An assassin **killed** the king last night).

The emphasis is placed on *killed*. If we wish to emphasize another part of this sentence, the word order is changed and the word to be emphasized is placed just ahead of the verb:

A királyt ölte meg tegnap este a bérgyilkos (**The king** was killed last night by an assassin).

Tegnap este ölte meg a királyt egy bérgyilkos (**Last night** was killed the king by an assassin).

Egy bérgyilkos ölte meg a királyt tegnap este (**An assassin** killed the king last night).

In Hungarian, the emphasis is always placed on the first syllable of a word. The consistency of this usage played an important role in the history of the language and in the evolution of the present Hungarian linguistic system. When the words are strung together to form a sentence, not every word has to be emphasized separately, but only those which are the leading words or the focus of the sentence (generally a new, important component). We call this the emphasized or focal part of the sentence and it represents the principal content of the sentence that we wish to convey.

Postpositional interrogative:
It is one of the peculiarities of the Hungarian language that an interrogative marker *(-e)* may be attached to a given word, usually to the verb or noun that is emphasized: *Van-e nálad térkép?* (Do you have a map?)

The order of names:
In every European language, the given name precedes the family name (John Smith), and it is only in Hungarian that the given name follows the family name *(Kovács János)*. This peculiar word order has a linguistic explana-

tion. The family name is an attribute, and generally a qualitative or possessive attribute. In most languages, the possessive attribute follows the indicated word. Thus the given name, also known as the first name, comes first and is then followed by the family name, also known as last name, e.g.: John Kennedy.

In the Hungarian language, the possessive attributive construction is exactly the reverse. First comes the possessor (attribute), and then the possessed (emphasized word), and therefore the sequence is reversed in the personal names: *Bartók Béla, Kodály Zoltán, Kossuth Lajos*. Hungarian linguistic terms reflect this and the given name is called the *utónév* ("aftername") or *keresztnév* (baptismal name). The term, first name, used in almost all other languages has to be translated into Hungarian as "after name".

Other than in Hungarian, this form of name usage occurs only in Japanese. The sequence of family name + given name has some practical significance. The names need not be reversed to be placed in alphabetical order. For the sake of convenience in alphabetizing, other languages reverse the order of the names as well, but in these instances, a comma is placed between the family name and the given name. This is occasionally referred to as the "Hungarian sequence".

Why don't we see the same system of names in the other Finno-Ugrian languages? It seems likely that they succumbed to the pressure of the surrounding Indo-European languages and that only the Hungarian language was able to withstand the pressure.

From the general to the specific:
It is a characteristic of the Hungarian language that it moves from the general, or larger units or concepts, to the more specific, or smaller units. This is reflected in the personal names: the family name (general, larger unit) is followed by the given name (specific).

The same holds for the Hungarian system of dating: year - month - day, e.g., *1997. január 1.* This is the way we find the date on the front page of the newspapers, in correspondence, etc. The full year designation may be abbreviated in Hungarian as well, such as '96.

The same scheme is followed in the precise time designation: hour - minute - second, e.g. 16 hours, 30 minutes 10 seconds. The telephone time signal uses the same system. (Like in other countries in Europe, the 24 hour clock is used in all official and much interpersonal communication.)

Addresses follow the same scheme, going from the larger to the smaller: *Budapest V. kerület, Váci utca 19. IV/5* (city, district, street, number, floor, door).

Numbers:

The composite numbers are expressed in Hungarian according to the rules of co-ordination and in the characteristic larger to smaller order. The numbers from one to ten have their individual names: *egy, kettő (két), három, négy, öt, hat, hét, nyolc, kilenc, tíz* (one, two, three, … ten).

Starting with 11, we find the general to specific progression, i.e., larger to smaller numeric terms: 11 - *tizenegy* (10+1), 15 - *tizenöt* (10+5), 20 - *húsz* (twenty), 25 - *huszonöt* (20+5), 100 - *száz* (hundred), 121 - *százhuszonegy* (100+20+1), 569 - *ötszázhatvankilenc* (500+60+9).

The cardinal number two:

There are two situations which bring to mind the existence of the cardinal number two in dual form. The two forms are **két** and **kettő** and the two are not interchangeable. *Két* is used only attributively for giving the number of a noun, etc. Thus: *két ház* (two houses). *Kettő* is used everywhere else and frequently indicates a duality, e.g.: *kettő helyett dolgozik* (he does the work of two people).

The other situation refers to the paired organs of the human body. In the Hungarian language these are ordinarily indicated by the singular. *Tördeli a kezét* (he wrings his hand[s]).

Under Indo-European influence, this system is becoming obsolete, and the use of plurals in this situation is becoming common: *tördeli a kezeit* (he wrings his hands).

The Hungarian text:

One can note a strong traditionalism in Hungarian texts. In most texts, there are relatively many stereotyped word groupings (expressions, proverbs, quotations), an extensive use of metaphors in the expressions and word formations, and a marked anthropomorphism, namely the attribution of human and animal characteristics, activities and body parts to living human beings. E.g.: *kabátujj* (coatfinger - sleeve), *szőlőszem* (grape-eye - grape), *repül az idő* (time flies), *nyakig van a bajban* (he is in trouble up to his neck).

The use of anecdotes is also an important component of Hungarian texts and so is the frequent use of rustic humor and jokes of all kinds. The word usage also reflects a certain mentality. One example: The American *makes* money, the French *wins* money *(gagner)*, the German *deserves* money *(verdient)*, the Russian acquires or *gathers* money *(sabirati)*, while the Hungarian *looks for* or *seeks* money *(keres)*.

Communicating in Hungarian:

There are two mutually contradictory beliefs concerning the speaking habits of the Hungarians. According to one, the Hungarian is taciturn and talks very little. There is even an expression which says: "The Hungarian does not speak while he eats." (This is generally untrue.) According to the other belief, the Hungarian is loquacious, verbose, and his rhetoric is flimsy. He has trouble distinguishing the important from the unimportant and hence his public utterances are frequently unstructured and faulty. We are evidently dealing with different societal manifestations. The Hungarian peasant was reluctant to speak for the record, and the gentlemen were very taciturn when questioned repeatedly. When they had to speak in an official capacity, it was difficult for them to express themselves in suitable, gentlemanly language. This actually may conceal some ancient national wisdom: "If my mouth stays shut, my head won't hurt" (*"Nem szól szám, nem fáj fejem"*).

Hungarian sentence melody:
According to Béla Bartók and Zoltán Kodály, the traditional Hungarian folksong has a descending-falling and dome-shaped ascending falling structure. This is reminiscent of Cheremis and Chuvash-Turkish folksongs. Hungarian and Turkish spoken emphasis and cadence perfectly reflects this descending trend. The traditional Hungarian communicational basic graph faithfully follows this structure. For this reason, there is no rise at the end of the sentence in Hungarian, except when the sentence is an open question.

Synthetic and analytic elements in Hungarian grammar:
The Hungarian language is fundamentally synthetic (creating dense constructs). It does have, however, some analytic elements as well:

synthetic:	*megyek, mennék* (I go, we would go)
analytic:	*mentem volna, menni fog* (I would have gone, he will go)
synthetic:	*elmegy* (he leaves)
analytic:	*el nem megy, megy el* (he's not leaving, he's leaving)
synthetic:	*Hallotta holtát* (He heard [about] his death)
analytic:	*Hallotta, hogy meg kell halnia* (He heard that he had to die)

The Uralian-Finno-Ugrian Kinship of the Hungarian Language

According to prevalent linguistic views, the Hungarian language may be assigned to the Ugrian branch of the Uralian-Finno-Ugrian family of languages. The nearest relatives to the Hungarian language at the present time are the Vogul and Ostyak languages spoken by about 10,000 people in Western-Siberia. More distant relatives are the Finnish and Estonian languages.

The concept of kinship with the Finno-Ugrian languages is approximately 1000 years old and the Finno-Ugrian theory was born about 200 years ago. It was accepted by the scientific community about 100 years ago. Its expansion into the Uralian-Finno-Ugrian kinship has been accepted only for the past 60 years. However, let us proceed in an orderly fashion.

The astronomer János Sajnovics published his *Demonstratio Idioma Hungarorum et Lapponum Idem Esse* in Copenhagen in 1770 (Demonstrating the identity of the Hungarian and Lappish languages). The publication in Göttingen, in 1799, of *Affinitas linguae Hungaricae cum linguis fennicae originis grammatice demonstrata* (The grammatical proof of the kinship of the Hungarian and Finnish languages) by the physician and professor Sámuel Gyarmathy included not only the Lappish language in his studies, but Finnish and even Samoyed, and demonstrated that there were similarities not only in their words but also in their grammatical structure.

Hungarian has generally been considered an Eastern language. Earlier, it was thought to be related to the great classic languages, Hebrew, Greek, Latin, Sanskrit and, according to one linguist, to English. Currently the weight of scientific evidence is in favor of a kinship with the Altaic (ancient Turkic and Chuvash) languages. There are also a few alternative attributions. In addition to the Turkish, Altaic Uygur, Indo-European Persian and Japanese have been considered. The Hungarian language has even been thought to be related to the Mid-Eastern and Near-Eastern languages, like the equally unique Sumerian and Egyptian.

During the second half of the 19th century, there were numerous debates in Hungarian scientific circles concerning the origin of the Hungarians and particularly concerning the Finno-Ugrian versus the Turkic linguistic relationships. Because of the vehemence of the debates, they were referred to as the "Ugrian-Turkish War", although the title "Ugrian-Hungarian War" may have been more appropriate since the Finno-Ugrian partisans were fighting with the partisans of all the other linguistic alternatives. Armin Vámbéry, the eminent Turkologist, stood at the head of the Turkish detachment and many major figures of the Hungarian intellectual circles were lined up behind him. The primary representatives of the Finno-Ugrian side were József Budenz and Pál Hunfalvy.

Such scientific debates are rapidly invaded by cultural politics and national pride. Finno-Ugrian lampoons appeared and the supporters of the Finno-Ugrian theory were accused of trying to trace the Hungarian origins back to riff-raff, reeking of fish-oil. Continued researches into the Altaic-Turkic theory and additional linguistic studies into the internal characteristics of the Hungarian language led to the conclusion, toward the end of the 19th century, that the Turkish theory was untenable, and since that time no further serious work has been done in this area.

A number of publications opposed to the Finno-Ugrian linguistic kinship have been published by Hungarians living in emigration after World War II (Ida Bobula, Ferenc Badinyi Jós, Tibor Baráth, László Götz). A number of these saw the light of day in Hungary after 1989 and have become the shuttle-cocks in political games. With only one or two exceptions, the Hungarian academic community has rejected these works and has labeld them unscientific and "without merit".

At the present time it is the generally accepted linguistic opinion that the Hungarian language belongs to the Uralian-Finno-Ugrian language family and is related to the languages belonging to this linguistic group.

The term 'Uralian' has been applied to this linguistic family since the 1960s. It suggests that the original home and the site where the Uralian tribes lived together was somewhere among the Ural mountains, i.e., on the eastern borders of Europe. The strongest proof for the Uralian original home being in Europe is the so-called *"méz"* (honey) argument. This is used in the same way as the "oak" argument is used for the Indo-European nations and the "mountain" argument is used for the Semitic nations. The principle of the "honey" argument is that all the Uralian languages have a common, ancient term to designate honey and bees. The honey-bee was not yet known at that time in Asia, and thus the site where these ancient tribes lived together had to be to the west of the Urals. The word *méz* has corresponding terms in the Indo-European languages and this somewhat weakens the Uralian theory (e.g.: Sanskrit *madhu*, Greek *methu*, Slav *medu* and German *Meet*). Yet, there are objective arguments which make it likely that the word has a Finno-Ugrian origin.

Finno-Ugrian is the older term applied to this linguistic family and is derived by linking the Finns and the Ugrians which are the two tribes geographically most remote from each other. The Uralian linguistic family may be divided into the Finno-Ugrian and Samoyed language groups. Among the Samoyed languages, we know of four which are still used, and several which have died out. According to the Uralian theory, the Samoyeds separated from the Uralian community about 4000 B.C. There are today approximately 30,000 Samoyed speaking people living in Siberia.

The other main branch of the Uralian linguistic family is the Finno-Ugrian. This in turn is divided into two groups, the Finnish and the Ugrian language groups. The living languages of the Finno-Permic group (named after the city of Perm) are: Finnish, Estonian, Lappish, Mordvin, Votyak (Udmurt), Zurjen (Komi) and Cheremis (Mari), as well as some smaller ones: Izhor, Vepse, Vot and Liv (some of these are spoken today only by a handful of people, but they are represented in Finno-Ugrian linguistic congresses). The languages of the Ugrian branch are: Vogul (Manysi) and Ostyak (Chanti). The latter are also known as the Ob-Ugrians, since currently they live along the Ob river and number approximately 10,000 people. Their nearest linguistic relative is the Hungarian language.

According to estimates, the total number of the Finno-Ugrian linguistic community is put at approximately 25 million of whom the majority – 15 million – speak Hungarian. In this entire group the Hungarian language has the oldest written and oral traditions.

Hungarians are asked frequently whether they understand the other Finno-Ugrian languages and whether they can follow a Finn, Estonian or Vogul speaking his own language. Are their languages closely enough related, like some Germanic languages, so that even a lay person interested in linguistics may detect similarities?

The people speaking the Finno-Ugrian languages do not understand each other and their kinship can be established only by expert linguistic researches. Vogul and Ostyak are about as close to each other as Slovakian and Czech, but they would not understand a single word of Hungarian. The kinship between Hungarian and Finnish is about as close as the "kinship" between English and Russian, albeit both of them are Indo-European languages. In other words, the kinship is a purely linguistic one and is completely obscure to the persons speaking either of the two languages. The linguists have created some sentences in the Finno-Ugrian languages which seem to resemble each other but such sentences would be most unusual in everyday conversation:

Finnish:	*Kala uiskele elävänä veden alla.*
Hungarian:	*Hal úszkál elevenen a víz alatt.*
English:	*Fish swims vivaciously under water.*

Vogul:	*Hurem-sat-hus hulach-sam uampen viten äli.*
Hungarian:	*Háromszázhúsz hollószemű ebem vizen él.*
English:	*Threehundred-twenty of my raven-eyed dogs live on the water.*

What are the linguistic proofs for the kinship of the Finno-Ugrian (Uralian) languages? Linguistic kinship means that in all areas of a language (phonetics, vocabulary, grammar, phraseology, etc.), there must be regular correspondence and trends, even though there are no true equalities. We can not speak of regular equalities or obvious similarities, since the Finno-Ugrian people separated from each other a long time ago, lived their own, independent lives, and their language evolved in isolation. A very long period of time will inevitably separate related languages. Those languages which separated rather late and remained in geographic proximity do not differ very much from each other (e.g.: Czech and Slovakian, Spanish and Portuguese, Finnish and Estonian).

The ancient languages, the so-called basic languages, spoken by all the people, are identified on the basis of the history of the language and on the basis of etymological studies, using comparative linguistic history and occurrence of the consistent correspondences of certain sounds. The sounds of the languages suspected of being related are examined to see whether there may be some phonetic consistency (correspondence) between them. The initial *p* sound was preserved in Finno-Ugrian and corresponds to the Hungarian *f*. Hence: the Finnish *pää* ≈ the Hungarian *fej* (head), the Finnish *puu* ≈ the Hungarian *fa* (wood or tree). In the basic Finno-Ugrian language, the initial *k* may be either *k* or *h* in Hungarian:

Finnish	Hungarian	English
käte	*kéz*	hand
kive	*kő*	stone
kala	*hal*	fish

The characteristic structure of the Finno-Ugrian stem words is: VCV, CVCV and CVCCV where C is a consonant and V is a vowel. In other words, the Hungarian language prefers vowels and consonants alternating as much as possible. Finnish preserved this to this day, while in Hungarian the final vowels have been lost. They can still be seen in some of our very earliest written material, e.g.: *utu* for *út* (road) and *türü* for *tőr* (dagger). The formulae show that in the Finno-Ugrian languages there was no duplication of consonants (CC) at the beginning of the words. This was true for Hungarian as well until the most recent times. E.g.: in medieval Latin the word *schola* (school) became the archaic *o-skola* and the modern *i-skola* in Hungarian and *koulu* in Finnish. It seems that the Hungarian has added a vowel and the Finnish has removed a consonant. It is an indication for the increasing Latinization (Indo-Europeanization) of the Hungarian language that recently it made no effort to eliminate the piling up of consonants. This is why we can now find words in the Hungarian language like *strand* (strand), *stréber* (pushing fellow), or the currently very popular abbreviation of *sztracsi* for the Italian ice cream *stracciatella*.

Evidence for the Hungarian language being part of the Finno-Ugrian family can be seen in the personal pronouns, in the verb conjugations derived from them, and in the possessive suffixes.

The Hungarian possessive suffixes *nő-m* (my woman), *kert-ed* (your garden), *ház-a* (his house), *vő-nk* (our son-in-law), *hajó-tok* (your, plural, boat) *kez-ük* (their hand) are all of Finno-Ugrian origin.

The majority of the verbal conjugation forms are also of Finno-Ugrian origin. E.g.: *lát-o-m* (I see it), *lát-o-d* (you see it), *lát-j-a* (he sees it) *lát-u-nk* (we see you) *lát-tok* (you, plural, see it).

Hungarian	Finnish	Lappish	Cheremish	English
én	minä	mon	min-	I
te	sinä	ton	tin	you
ő	hän	son	–	he-she-it
mi	me	mi	me	we
ti	te	di	te	you
ők	he	si	–	they

The sign for the imperative: *-j* ≈ ír-j (write!), for the conditional, *-na* (and its variants: *-ne/-ná,/-né*): ír-na (he would write), for the narrative past: *-á/-é:* ír-á (he had written) and the comparative: *-b/-bb:* külön-b (better) *fénylő-bb* (shinier), are all considered to be derived from the Finno-Ugrian.

In Finnish, Lappish, Vogul and Hungarian, the emphasis is on the first syllable. In the Finno-Ugrian languages there is no possessive structure like the *"habeo"* system in the Indo-European languages. E.g.: The Latin: *habeo librum*, the German: Ich habe ein Buch or the English: I have a book. Instead, in Hungarian the substantive verb, to be, is used in combination with the possessed word and a personal suffix: *van könyvem* (I have a book).

After a numeral, the Finno-Ugrian languages use only a singular: *tíz ember* (ten men), *öt mázsa szén* (five tons of coal).

There is no gender or grammatical agreement between the attribute and the word qualified by an adjective: e.g.: *okos embert* (a smart man).

The most comprehensive characteristic of these related languages is the synthetic, unifying sentence structure. These languages build what they have to say on single significant words and compress these into complex units. "Empty" words, such as auxiliary verbs which can not stand by themselves, and pronouns are rarely used. In contrast, the Indo-European languages break up what they have to say and make analytic constructions utilizing several auxiliary words. Let's take this sentence as an example: *Holtodiglan szeretnélek.* In German, this would read: *Ich würde dich bis zu deinem Tode lieben.* In English, we would say: *I would love you until the day you die.*

The very dense construction can be illustrated by the sign seen occasionally on week-end cottages: *Ötünké* (the full sentence would read: *Ez az ötünk tulajdona*). This complex relationship can be expressed in any Indo-European language only by a lengthy explanation:

Dutch:	*Dit/Deze is van ons vyven.*
German:	*Dieses Haus gehört uns fünfen.*
English:	*This house belongs to the five of us.*

In the Finno-Ugrian languages, the syntethizing characteristics are allied to a conjugational (agglutinative) construction. These languages are agglutinative according to their specific type and structural techniques. The relationship within the sentence is determined by the elements and suffixes attached to the words. The Indo-European languages either change the form of the word: e.g.: Latin: *res, rem, rei* ≈ Hungarian *a dolog, a dolgot, a dolognak a…,* English: *foot-feet,* Hungarian: *láb, lábak,* or use an auxiliary before or after the word (e.g.: German: *in meinem Haus,* English: *in my house,* Hungarian: *házamban*).

In addition to Hungarian, definite conjugation exists in our nearest linguistic relatives, the Vogul, the Östyak, the Mordvin and the Samoyed. In Ostyak, the definite conjugation may be used only when the object referred to in the conjugation is well known to the speaker, if it had been mentioned previously and if it is something that can be pointed out by a finger or by the nod of the head. The Hungarian definite conjugation follows broadly similar principles. The definite conjugation must be applied to known, specific and previously mentioned items. E.g.: *István, ott a másik szobában látsz egy könyvet. Látod? Hozd ide.* (István, there in the other room you see a book. Do you see it? Bring it here.)

In the first sentence, the conjugation is indefinite *(látsz),* since it deals with a book that has not been identified more specifically. The conjugation in the second sentence is definite *(látod),* since it refers to that specific book. The verb in the third sentence *(hozd ide)* is also definite, since it applies to the same previously identified book. The second and the third sentence could not stand by themselves since we would not know what was to be seen or fetched. (We would not know the specific item it referred to).

The Hungarian language has approximately 700 stem word which are considered to be Finno-Ugrian. This means that a word considered to be or suspected of being related will be contained in one of the Finno-Ugrian languages. The hoard of words which actually exists in all of the Finno-Ugrian languages is not very large. The hoard of stem words includes the most basic linguistic designations and terms. Such are the basic activities, the verbs meaning existence, pronouns, the names of body parts, kinship terms, the terms for natural phenomena and a few plant and animal names.

Pronouns: *én* (I), *te* (you), *ő* (he/she), *mi* (we), *ti* (you), *ez* (this), *az* (that), *ilyen* (such), *így* (so).

Simple numbers: *egy* (one), *kettő* (two), *három* (three), *négy* (four), *öt* (five), *hat* (six), *hét* (seven), *-ven (negy-ven)* (forty), *-van (hat-van)* (sixty), *száz* (hundred), *fél* (half), *első* (first).

Body parts: *fej* (head), *velő* (brain), *homlok* (forehead), *szem* (eye), *fül* (ear), *száj* (mouth), *aj-(ajak)* (lip), *nyelv* (tongue), *íny* (gums), *fog* (tooth). Hungarian *szem* (eye), Ostyak *szem*, Vogul *sem*, Zurjen *szijn*, Votjak *szjim*, Cheremish *szindsze*, Mordvin *szeljnje*, Finnish *silmä*, Lappish *chialm*.

Kinships: *atya* (father), *anya* (mother), *fiú* (son), *öcs* (younger brother), *árva* (orphan), *férfi* (man), *nő* (woman), *vő* (son-in-law).

Natural phenomena: *ég* (sky), *menny* (firmament), *világ* (world), *villám* (lightning), *csillag* (star), *hajnal* (dawn), *ősz* (fall), *tél* (winter), *tavasz* (spring), *víz* (water), *jég* (ice), *hó* (snow), *fagy* (freeze), *hegy* (mountain), *domb* (hill).

Animals: *daru* (crane), *fecske* (swallow), *fogoly* (partridge), *holló* (crow), *lúd* (goose), *hal* (fish), *keszeg* (bream).

Plants: *gyökér* (root), *tő* (stem), *kéreg* (bark), *vessző* (branch), *fa* (tree), *fürt* (bunch), *fagyal* (privet), *fűz* (willow), *fenyő* (pine), *nyír* (poplar).

Minerals: *kő* (stone), *vas* (iron), *arany* (gold), *ezüst* (silver), *ón* (tin), *ólom* (lead).

Home and tools: *ház* (house), *fal* (wall), *lak (lakik)* (lives), *ajtó* (door), *ágy* (bed), *fúró* (drill), *kés* (knife), *fen* (hone), *köszörül* (sharpen), *falu* (village), *nyereg* (saddle), *kengyel* (stirrup).

Nutrition: *fazék* (pot), *lé* (juice), *köles* (millet), *kenyér* (bread), *fő* ([it is] cooking), *süt* (bake), *eszik* (eats), *iszik* (drinks).

Action: *lesz* (will be), *él* (lives), *hal* (dies), *alszik* (sleeps), *áll* (stands), *fúj* (blows), *mond* (says), *hall* (hears), *néz* (looks), *lát* (sees), *fejt* (solves), *folyik* (it flows), *szül* (gives birth), *szív* (inhales, sucks), *hajlik* (leans).

Other: *csók* (kiss), *enek* (song), *had* (army), *haszon* (profit), *igen* (yes), *lélek* (soul), *név* (name), *szag* (odor), *ügy* (affair), *zaj* (noise), *magyar* (Hungarian).

An occasional ancient stem word has expanded into a very large family of words in the independent life of the Hungarian language. E.g.: of the original *el* noun (stem root) the following very extensive family of words has originated: *elé* (ahead of), *eleve* (in advance), *elő* (fore), *előre* (to the fore), *előd* (predecessor), *előtti* (former), *előbb* (prior to), *elöl* (in front), *elül* (in front), *elülről* (from the beginning), *elülső* (first), *elem* (element), *elemi* (elemental), *elemez* (analyze), *ellen* (against), *ellenség* (enemy), *ellenkezik* (protest), *ellenez* (oppose), *elnök* (president), *elnököl* (preside), *elnökség* (presidency), *előleg* (advance), *előlegez* (to advance), *előny* (advantage), *elv* (principle), *elvi* (a matter of principle), *elvszerű* (according to principles), *elég* (sufficient), *(meg)elégedik* (is satisfied), elégedetlen (dissatisfied), *(ki)elégített* (satisfied), *elegendő* (sufficient), *eléggé* (sufficiently), *elégtelen* (insufficient, unsatisfactory), etc.

A Hungarian linguist has made some calculations and found that in the currently spoken and written Hungarian the words of Finno-Ugrian origin and the words created internally were in such a majority that this constituted absolute proof for the Finno-Hungarian descent of the Hungarian language.

```
                    eléggé
              (ki)elégít  elegendő
           (meg)elégedik  elégedetlen

        elv      elvi    elvszerű      elég

     előz    előzetes   előzékeny   előzmény

        előtt     előtti    előbb      elől

  elem    elemi    elé    eleve   elő-    elül   elülről

     elemez    előd    EL-    előre    elülső

  ellen   előget  eleinte  elnök  elnökség

  ellenség  ellenkezik  ellenez  elnököl

        előleg   előlegez   előleges

           előny   előnyös

              előttemez

               elégtelen

                 stb.
```

Figure 3. The family of the stem-root word *el-*

Even a cursory examination will find a number of similarities among the Finno-Ugrian languages. The Hungarian says: *he died*, or *drowned into the water.* In other words, the Hungarian drowns into something and not in something, as for instance the German: *Im Wasser sterben.* In other Finno-Ugrian languages the same usage pertains and the drowning is directional, just as in Hungarian:

Cheremis: *wodes kolese* (died into water)
Finnish: *kuoli veteen* (he died into the water)

There are other examples for such linguistic-metaphysical manifestations. The Hungarian pulls his cap *into* his head (rather than *onto*), he says that the food is burning *to* (something), i.e., the pot, that he goes *with* a boat (rather than *on*), and that he becomes insane *into* something or someone (not *over* or *because of* something or someone). All these expressions show a kinship between Hungarian and the other Finno-Ugrian languages which see and express reality differently, more dynamically, directed toward something and belonging to something. The representatives of the Indo-European languages tend to see a condition and a merely static condition. This actually is a remarkably fine example of what the American anthropologic linguists Sapir and Whorf have termed linguistic relativism.

Apologists for Finno-Ugrian linguistic kinship naturally focus primarily on the similarities and de-emphasize the differences. It is nevertheless a fact that there are very great differences between the various Finno-Ugrian languages. A Finno-Ugrian linguist examined 20 grammatical characteristics in eight Uralian languages. There was not a single one that was present identically in all of them. It appeared that the common characteristics were a function of geographic proximity rather than of linguistic kinship. Thus, e.g.: Permian–Cheremis, Finnish–Lappish, Mordvin–Cheremis and Samoyed-Ob-Ugrian. According to this study, Hungarian had the greatest grammatical affinity with Permian, Mordvin and Cheremis.

In some related languages (Samoyed, Ob-Ugrian and Lappish) we can find a "dual" number which takes its place between the number one referring to individual items and the number three that refers to more than one item. There is some question whether this dualism really existed in the original Uralian root language although similar grammatical curiosities can be found in Greek, Gothic and some Slavic languages.

The great differences between the Uralian-Finno-

Ugrian languages partly date back to ancient times, but are mainly the result of having been separated geographically for a long time. Even the agglutinative techniques are no longer unique to all Finno-Ugrian languages.

Uralian linguistics will probably give rise to numerous debates and the linguistic and non-linguistic origin of these people undoubtedly still holds many secrets.

The theory of Finno-Ugrian linguistic kinship, based on the findings of philology, leads to much discussion of Finno-Ugrian family relationships, which in turn is leading to the development of a "Finno-Ugrian identity". They are talking not only of the linguistic kinship of the Finno-Ugrian people, but of their common history, folklore, folk music and literature. Every five years a Finno-Ugrian World Congress is organized, there are bilateral Finno-Ugrian friendship societies, and more recently a Finno-Ugrian youth organization has been formed, all of which foster and nurture the idea of a Finno-Ugrian identity.

Are the Hungarians Finno-Ugrians?
Is There a Single Source or Are There
Multiple Sources?

According to the evidence of Finno-Ugrian linguistic theory, the Hungarians are Uralian-Finno-Ugrians. It must be emphasized, however, that the Finno-Ugrian theory is only a linguistic theory and thus is suitable only for the reconstruction of linguistic kinships. In the absence of the necessary historic, archaeological and other proofs, reconstructive linguistic theory was used to prove historic, ethnic and cultural kinships as well as "origin". It certainly can not be excluded and may even be a logical assumption that those who speak related languages have a common origin, yet being familiar with the variously strong linguistic interactions and even with the exchange of languages, this is by no means the only possible explanation. It may well be considered that within the Finno-Ugrian theory, the Hungarians are the largest group among the Uralian peoples, the ones who migrated the farthest, the ones who represent about two-thirds of the total of 25 million, and that they are the people with the oldest written records. A number of the smaller Finno-Ugrian peoples became literate only in the 19th and 20th centuries.

The Finno-Ugrian theory furnishes only a single and apparently incomplete answer to the origin of the Hungarians. In their anthropological appearance, the Hungarians, even at first glance, are completely different than their closest relatives, the Ob-Ugrians. According to the anthropologists, present-day Hungarians carry only 6% Ugrian characteristics. In contrast, there is a very high incidence of Turkic, Turanian and Taurid, as well as Iranian, Pamiri and Taurid anthropological characteristics. There are many theories about the history of the Hungarians. The medieval chroniclers were unanimous in recording a Scythian-Hun origin. Hungarian folklorist and musical affinities also led the researchers toward different people (mostly Altaic).

This of course does not mean unequivocally that the Hungarians cannot be Finno-Ugrians. They are that linguistically, even allowing for the fact that other linguistic reconstructions are possible. If the Hungarians belong among the Finno-Ugrians linguistically (and this is the currently accepted theory), it does not necessarily mean that the Hungarians are Finno-Ugrians. With today's methodology, a Finno-Ugrian culture can be created but can not be reconstructed.

Who then are the Hungarians?

This question can be answered only by someone who has excessive self-confidence. Written records do not completely illuminate the ancient history, since they mention a number of Asiatic people who at times lived together and then separated and who are known by a variety of names. The data surviving from our early history can not always be precisely identified with any given people. The Hungarians reached their present home in the Carpathian Basin from the east, from Asia and, presumably, from Central-Asia. They traveled back and forth on the "highway" of the most highly developed equestrian people and followed their own logic in so doing.

The historians studying our ancient history relied for the longest time on the linguistic, reconstructive methodology and accepted the presumptive kinship based on purely linguistic data.

The original homeland:

According to the prehistory derived from the Finno-Ugrian linguistic theory, the history of the Hungarians reaches back to the Uralian "settlement area" approximately 6,000 years ago. In the 6th to 4th millennia, B.C., the Uralian "family of people" (perhaps the Uralian branch of the Ural-Altaic family) hunted fished and gathered among the central and southern reaches of the Ural mountains. In the 4th millennium B.C., the Samoyeds migrated to the east, separated from the Finno-Ugrians and brought an end to the Uralian community. The Finno-Ugrians remaining in the area lived along the Volga, Oka and Kama rivers in the western reaches of the Urals. According to one theory the "Finno-Ugrian Unity" broke up at the end of the 3rd millennium, B.C., with the separation of the Finnish and Permian people. The Ugrians, and among them the proto-Hungarians wandered in a southerly and south-easterly direction to the Tobol and Irtis river basins, perhaps into the area of the present city of Chelyabinsk. It is here that they met with the ancient Iranian people, the Sarmatae and developed jointly, the so-called Andronovo culture. It was between 2000 and 1500 B.C., that they abandoned their plunder economy and switched to the production of food (agriculture and animal husbandry), and also developed an advanced metal-working technology.

The "Ugrian symbiosis" broke up between 1300 and 1000 B.C., largely because of climatic changes (warming and a shift of the steppe belt toward the north). At this time the Vogul and the Ostyak, still committed primarily to hunting and fishing, moved to the north into Western-Siberia and settled along the Ob river. Hence their present name of Ob-Ugrians. The ancestors of the Hungarians adapted to the changing conditions and switched to a nomadic, pastoral animal husbandry and to commerce. Thus the appearance of the ancient Hungarians and the independent existence of the Hungarian language is placed at about 1000 B.C. by the experts. It was at this time as well that the Hungarians established close relationships with the Scythian tribes who ruled this area.

The first – reconstituted – "original homeland" was probably at the southern edge of the Ural mountains, from whence the early Hungarians migrated to the western part of the Urals. In 463 A.D., they were living in an

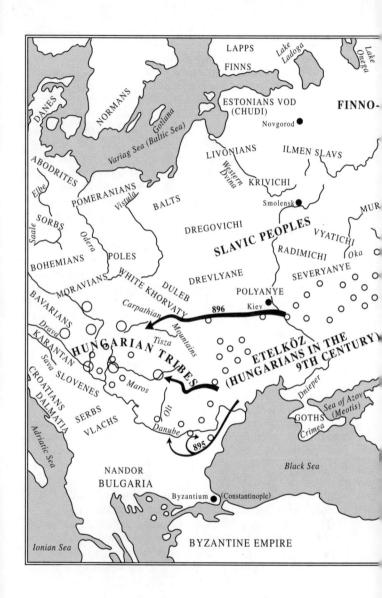

Figure 4. The Uralian-Finno-Ugrian original home and the migrations of the Hungarians

area bordered by the Volga, Kama and Belaja rivers. This area is today's Baskiria (a part of Russia). It was later designated as Magna Hungaria since Hungarians were encountered here even centuries later.

Their next area of settlement was in Levedia, in an area between the lower Volga, the Don, the Donec and the Sea of Azov where they joined the ethnically and linguistically mixed Onogur association. From 650, they were part of the Kazar Empire (Kaganate). Because of internal fights in the empire, the Hungarians moved to the area between the rivers Dnyeper, Dnyester, Seret and the lower Danube. In their own language, this area between the rivers was known as *Etelköz*. From this time on, the fighting Hungarians were frequently invited by German princes engaged in internecine warfare and this gave the Hungarians the opportunity of becoming familiar with Europe. Because of some Pecheneg attacks, the conquest of the Carpathian Basin was a carefully planned campaign, which took place under the leadership of Árpád in 895-896. Later on the Hungarians invited and accepted the Petchenegs in the Carpathian Basin.

According to the linguists and to the official historians, Hungarian ancient history can be outlined as above.

Other models:
The medieval Hungarian chronicles and gestes uniformly held that the Hungarians were related to the Scythians and to the Huns. There are several data which suggest that the Hungarians encountered familiar people in the Carpathian Basin. After the Romans had left, only three nations managed to establish a strong country in the Carpathian Basin. These were the Huns, who probably spoke a Turkic language, the Avars who spoke an unknown language, which may have been Turkic and the Hungarians. These three nations almost certainly had established contact previously, still in Asia. After the slow disintegration of Attila's empire, the Avars reached the Carpathian

86

Basin in 568. The Hungarian chroniclers avoid any mention of them and speak only of the Huns and of the Hungarians. They also mention, that sometimes around 670 "white Ogurs" arrived in the Carpathian Basin. They probably omit mentioning the Avars because they were very close to the Hungarians in culture and language. The archaeological findings prove that at the time of the Hungarian conquest (895-896), at the end of the 9th century no radically new culture appeared in the Carpathian Basin. This is the basis of the dual or multiple conquest theory represented by Gyula László. Thus, the first conquest by the Hungarians, their predecessors and related tribes took place several hundred years earlier (according to some around 600 or 670). The old chroniclers refer to the 895-896 conquest as a "return" or as a "move back".

The Hun-Hungarian theory has numerous supporters. It was taught in the schools until the 19th century, and it has been only since then that under the influence of the Finno-Ugrian theory, public opinion has rejected the older theory. The credibility of the chroniclers is seriously questioned by their "search for a glorious past" and by their conscious attempt at mythologizing the past. Yet the medieval chroniclers were much closer to the origins and to the conquest. It is characteristic of the Asiatic nomadic people that they can name their ancestors very precisely and going back for several centuries. The newer Avar-Hungarian kinship theory is becoming increasingly accepted in scientific circles. In the light of this, it may be appropriate to re-examine the "straight-line" Uralian-Finno-Ugrian linguistic and historic descent.

There are numerous indications that thanks to their equestrian-nomadic way of life the Hungarians divided into several groups. Consequently, it may be more accurate to talk about Hungarian nations. Hungarians lived in Baskiria at least until 1236, since the envoy of King Béla IV, brother Julianus met them there. Julianus was a Dominican brother, who found Hungarian speaking people in 1235 and then again in 1237 along the Volga (Etil) river, in an area, he referred to as "Magna Hungaria" and believed to be the original home of the Hungarians. He brought news to Béla IV of these eastern Hungarians and also of the great Mongolian peril threatening Europe. This did materialize and in 1241, swept away Magna Hungaria and half of the Hungary in the Carpathian Basin. It was only at the line of the Danube that the Tatar advance came to a stop.

There are other indications that the Hungarians had divided into several groups. In the Vatican Archives there are data showing that in 1329, Pope John XXII appointed a certain Tamás as Catholic bishop to the Hungarians along the river Kuna. This is along the Caspian Sea in the northern regions of the Caucasus, an area of massive national and linguistic intermingling, where there are Chechens, Kalmuks, Karachay, Uygurs, Balkars, Ossetes, Armenians, and others living even today. In the collective memory of some of these people (Armenians and Chechens) there is presently a vivid recollection that a long time ago they lived side by side with the ancient Hungarians. The Hungary along the Kuma was destroyed by the Mongolian troops of Timur Lenk in 1395-96.

The Hungarians, divided into several groups and over several areas, were moving both east and west and during these forays came into contact with numerous small groups of people, who were never even identified in their own empires and who have left no historic memorials of their existence. Turkic, and secondarily Iranian fragments were alloyed to the Hungarians. Together, we refer to these people as "satellite nations", or as the eastern components of the Hungarians. A true reconstruction of these events is not possible.

The Hungarian-Turkic (Altaic) linguistic kinship has been dropped from the agenda of the official linguistic sciences, but the question of "kinship" can nevertheless be raised legitimately. The persistent contacts between the two peoples, may serve as the basis of further linguistic affinity studies. A number of cultural and linguistic parallels draw the investigators toward the Turkic nations. The Hungarian and the Turkic (Altaic) people (Bulgarian-Turks, Chuvash, Uygurs, Kazars and the Huns and Avars) lived in close proximity for centuries and intermingled during these years. Archaeological excavations have found Turkic artifacts in both Avar graves and also in graves dating back to the conquest. At the time of the conquest, the Hungarians arrived in the Carpathian Basin, accompanied by Turkic tribes and, according to some, under the leadership of Turkic aristocrats. We find the ancient pentatonic structure in both the Hungarian and Turkic folk music. Linguistic science emphasizes the large percentage of Turkic words among the accessory words acquired before the conquest. According to a more recent assumption, there are about 1,500 related words in the Turkish and Hungarian language.

The Turkish-Hungarian cultural and linguistic parallels are generally explained as geographic contacts, but it is possible that we are dealing with more than this. During the past century, Ármin Vámbéry worked out a singe convergence theory to explain the dual linguistic kinship. In his work, *A magyarok eredete* (The Origin of the Hungarians, 1882), he believes that the basis and the kernel of the Hungarian language and people is Turkish and that the Finno-Ugrian lines were secondary. Later he reversed his point of view and his original ideas never became the official tenet. Yet, it is clear that after the Uralian-Finno-Ugrian linguistic kinship, the Altaic (Turkish) linguistic kinships and theories deserve the highest attention.

Lajos Kazár extended the path derived from the Uralian philology all the way to a Hungarian-Japanese linguistic kinship. He proves a Hungarian-Japanese connection for 594 word families and claims that among the Uralian languages Hungarian shows the greatest affinity for the Japanese. Just like in Hungarian, there are a number of word groupings in Japanese that divide (split) into several branches.

The following common root words suggest an ancient Finno-Ugrian (Uralian) - Indo-European linguistic kinship: *víz* (water), *ház* (house), *szer* (implement), *ág* (branch), *fazék* (pot). Words common with the ancient Iranian include: *arany* (gold), *ár* (price), *hét* (seven), *ostor* (whip). The word *méz* (honey) is clearly derived from the Finno-Ugrian.

In the present century there was a rash of advocates for a Sumerian-Hungarian linguistic kinship. Sumerian was spoken in southern Mesopotamia and very many written documents survive, but Sumerian has absolutely no kinship to any language currently alive. Naive, "fata morgana" chasing linguistic kinship seekers ignore the evolutional principles of a language, comparing 3,000 year old Sumerian words with currently used Hungarian word forms. Even though there may be a surprising similarity between some of these words, serious linguists refuse to accept such artificial word associations which completely ignore the evolutional trends of modern languages. Since Sumerian has been a dead language, the words have to be viewed as permanent and unchanging.

Sumerian	Hungarian	English
bur	*fúr*	drill
ibilu	*ifjú*	youngster
kiel	*hely*	place
gir	*sarló*	sickle
gur	*súly*	weight
ná	*nő*	woman
dulu	*dal*	song
izzi	*izzik*	glow
edin	*edény*	pan
kus	*hús*	meat

Kálmán Gosztonyi (1975) studied 53 Sumerian grammatical characteristics and concluded that 21 of these have parallels in the Finno-Ugrian languages, 29 in Turkish, 51 in Hungarian, 24 in the Caucasian languages, 7 in Polynesian, 8 in the Paleosiberian, 12 in Tibetan-Burmese, 9 in the Munda language, 5 in Sanskrit, Akkadian, Dravidian and Chinese, 4 in Basque and other Indo-European languages. He related about 60% of 1,000 Sumerian words (roots and suffixes) to Hungarian.

Tibor Baráth published his work *A magyar népek őstörténete* (Ancient History of the Hungarian People) in three volumes in Montreal (1968-1974). In this he derives Hungarian from the Egyptian.

There are even some theories today which claim that "the Hungarians are the original settlers of the Carpathian Basin" and that "the Hungarian language was an original language, and was 90% Hungarian in background". In a study entitled Tamana doctrine, Bátor Tóth Vámos, living in Hawaii, tries to prove that the geographical designations of the Polynesian islands, and indeed of the entire globe, are of Hungarian origin. In recent times László Szabédi, once again raised the issue of the Latin-Hungarian linguistic kinship.

It seem clear that neither linguistics nor archaeology by themselves will guide us back to the ancient history of the Hungarians. There is an obvious need for a research project that covers all of Eurasia. The results of the Sinologists and Turkologists must be integrated with the researches of the Finno-Ugrian linguists. Some threads lead to Inner Asia, others to the region of the Caucasus where so many strong ethnic and cultural influences converged from the east and from the south. These two geographic areas probably hold the "key" to Hungarian ancient history. We can thus but reiterate, in connection with the Hungarian language, that *Hungary is Eurasia in miniature.*

The numerous theories and theory modifications strongly suggest that we may not talk about a "straight line" development and that the data of the archaeologists, historians, geographers and linguists must be set into a logical framework. The assumption that Hungarian is an independent primary language is patently naive. Yet, narrowing the linguistic kinships too much is also worrisome. The Hungarian language is almost certainly a language of several roots. Living and mingling with a variety of peoples and smaller ethnic groups, (mainly Iranian and Finno-Ugrian), may well have resulted in a form of a composite "caravan-language" as we have seen in Africa. It is almost certainly incorrect to apply our current linguistic knowledge to the languages spoken by the nomadic societies. Even though the Asiatic nomads had a well developed culture, one may not assume the existence of a "simple" language. Yet, population densities were low, there were numerous changes in location, symbiosis with a variety of people was common, while others were subjugated. All this suggests that the language was probably grammatically somewhat imprecise. Instead of speaking of a language it may be more accurate to speak of a linguistic chain reflecting a linguistic adaptation of the languages of the people living in close proximity. "The Hungarian languages" may have evolved gradually as just such communicational instruments. Naturally, there may have been several linguistic exchanges and thus there may possibly be some foundation for the alternative theories.

The results of the Finno-Ugrian linguistic studies are absolutely firm as far as the linguistic history, linguistic kinships and contacts are concerned. The Uralian languages have additional and much farther-reaching "outlets". Beyond the Ural-Altaic, they are alleged to be related to Eskimo, and Japanese, and even the "immense" family, i.e., an Uralian-Indo-European linguistic kinship is postulated. In the final analysis probably all languages go back to one or more basic languages and we will never have a truly accurate answer. Yet, perhaps we were able to clear up a few questions raised by the last few thousand years of linguistic history.

Without Linguistic Memorials. The Birth of the Hungarian Language (1000 B.C. - 896 A.D.)

Thus, according to the Uralian-Finno-Ugrian theory, the Hungarian language and its Finno-Ugrian relatives have a history that can be traced back 6-7 thousand years. This makes the Hungarian language and its European relatives the oldest, continuously used, primary languages in Europe. The emergence and history of the independent Hungarian language can be dated to the breaking up of the Ugrian linguistic community, approximately around the year 1000 B.C. There are no linguistic survivals, dating back to this so-called ancient Hungarian period, except for a few runic inscriptions. Hungarian runic script (about which more later) has southern and eastern connections. Hungarian runic script is not identical with the Old German runes which developed about 100 B.C. and were used along the shores of the Baltic. The appearance of the Hungarian language and its gaining its independence represents the longest single linguistic historical event and can be studied only indirectly by a reconstructive technique. Shortly after the original, ancient period Latin characters appear, become widely used and replace the runic writing. From the 16th century on, the so-called middle Hungarian period, we have printed material. Linguistic history refers to the period before the conquest as one without a linguistic record and to the period after the conquest as one having abundant written memorials. Thus according to the Uralian-Finno-Ugrian point of view, the Ugrian symbiotic period came to an end about 1000 B.C. and this signaled the beginning of the evolution of the independent Hungarian, Vogul and Ostyak languages and peoples. The precise spot where this independence was achieved has not been determined, but it most likely took place somewhere in the southern foothills of the Ural mountains. The migrations were caused by pressures from the east and by overpopulation among the local tribes.

The closest linguistic relatives, the Vogul and the Ostyak, crossed the Urals, while the Hungarians were pushed toward the west by the pressure of various nomadic tribes. Along this "trip" lasting almost 2,000 years the Hungarians traded with a number of other tribes, lived with them, settled among them, mingled with them and divided into several groups.

Most ancient historians agree that the "Conquering Hungarians" started in Magna Hungaria (the present Baskiria; in medieval Latin *magna* meant ancient), and passed through Levedia and the Etelköz. From an archaeological perspective, there are affinities between the remains of the conquering Hungarians and the 6th-10th century Baskirian findings. The Hungarians probably appeared in this region about 463 A.D. What, if anything is left of the Magna Hungaria linguistic tradition? In two Baskirian root words we can recognize the Hungarian *Jenő* and *Gyarmat* root words and a number of Baskirian river names seem to have a Hungarian origin. In Levedia (*Dentü-Mogyer*) they lived as a part of the Kazar Empire, and moved from there to the *Etelköz* from where they finally reached the Carpathian Basin.

According to a written record that seems to apply to the Hungarians, the first Hungarian (*Onogur*) tribe entered the Carpathian Basin around 670. Following this, wave after wave of Hungarians entered this area. In the second half of the 800s they conducted four campaigns across this area, toward the west, on behalf of different western rulers. The fifth trip, in 895-896 was the true conquest or, according to ancient documents the "re-conquest". The conquerors came in several groups, from at least two directions, as a tribal association, presumably accompanied by Turkish or Kazar speaking people and finding other people in the Carpathian Basin who had a similar (identical?) culture and language (*Avar* remnants).

According to tradition, seven Hungarian tribes participated in this "second" conquest (*Nyék, Megyer, Kürtgyarmat, Tarján, Jenő, Kér, Keszi*) and they were joined by three Kabar tribes (Turkish-speaking *Kazar* rebels) (*Várkony, Tárkány* and *Varsány*).

We must also mention the *Székely*s, who according to the chronicles, were Hungarian speaking people living in Transylvania, prior to the conquest. According to another theory, the *Székely*s are a separate tribe who joined the Hungarians and who were assigned border guard duties by the Hungarian rulers. In the area inhabited by the Hungarians there are many settlements the name of which incorporates the tribal names. Thus there are 25 *Nyék*s, 30 *Megyer*s, 21 *Kürt*s, 19 *Gyarmat*s, 14 *Tarján*s, 25 *Jenő*s, 41 *Kér*s and 40 *Keszi*s. There are also settlement names that recall the *Kabar*s, *Várkony, Tárkány* and *Varsány* as well as settlements incorporating the name *Székely*.

In Hungarian public opinion, the 896 conquest is the official one. It was the 1000th anniversary (millennium) of this date that was celebrated in 1896. For this occasion there was a major exposition in Budapest, a model of the Transylvanian Vajdahunyad Castle was erected, numerous public buildings were built, the Sugár út (today's *Andrássy út*) was finished and under it the first continental subway was built (London had one a few years earlier). Heroes' Square was established with the millennial monument and with the statues of the Hungarian kings. It was also this event that occasioned the creation of Árpád Feszty's monumental, romantic panorama of the conquest.

The ancient Hungarians represented a group of approximately 400 thousand people. Such a huge mass of people could not have survived without direction from above, organization, a solid background in domestic industries and a thorough understanding of agriculture. For the sake of comparison, it is of interest to look at the non-Latinized people of Europe at the end of the 800s. There are no great cities and there is no significant art. It is in this period that the neo-Latin and modern Germanic languages develop. As far as language was concerned Árpád's people did not differ much from the other European people. It was in their way of life and culture, however, that they proved to be a very different, hitherto unknown people indeed.

During the campaigns following the conquest, a prayer was frequently heard in western and southern Europe: *"De sagittis Hungarorum libera nos Domine"* (Lord, save us from the arrows of the Hungarians). Regino, the Abbot of Prün wrote: "They don't cut many down with their swords, but they kill that many more with their arrows... They can't fight for a long time, since if their endurance were as strong as their attack, they would be totally insupportable." Among many other items of information, Liutprand, the bishop of Cremona, in his work written between 959 and 962 describes the battle cry of the Hungarians, and this is the first record of a Hungarian interjection: *"turpis et diabolica hui, hui, frequenter auditur"* ("A hideous and diabolic yell of *hui, hui,* could frequently be heard").

These same Hungarians also understood agriculture and were already using the heavy plows along the Mediterranean, when this implement was still unknown in the rest of Europe. They used breast harness on their horses and shod them which represented a revolution in cartage. In the approximately 2000 years how did the fate of the independent Hungarian language evolve? In addition to historic and cultural influences the words themselves bear testimony to this. The inherited, original Finno-Ugrian word hoard of the Hungarian language includes approximately 700 ancient root words.

Present-day Hungarian seems to suggest that the Hungarian people have separated from the Finno-Ugrians and had contacts with a number of other nations. The linguistic traces of these contacts lie in the loan-words (borrowed words) which one of the languages has taken over from another one. Naturally the symbiosis and intermingling resulted in a number of effects and for this reason it is not always possible to determine unequivocally the nature, strength and effects of the cultural-linguistic forces. We present only those loan-words which have been so recognized by our official linguistic history. Yet, as part of the more recent attempts to establish a variety of linguistic kinships, the status of the loan-words may undergo a sudden change. In fact, the loan-words may turn out to be original words, belonging to the vocabulary of one of the peoples or subgroups which were in intimate contact with the Hungarian people.

In assessing the ancient Hungarian and old Hungarian loan-words, let us examine some of the techniques used in etymology. Linguists refer to a word as a loan-word only if it has been assimilated into the new language and its foreign origins are no longer apparent in their spontaneous use in the adoptive language. The "strangeness" of a foreign word is still obvious. Similarity of words may be purely coincidental. There are probably no languages in the world in which we could not find at least a hundred words that sound similar and may, perhaps, even have a similar meaning. The Hungarian *ház*, allegedly has no kinship whatever to the German *Haus* or the English *house* even though they all sound similar. (Péter Sára derives it from the Turkish.) The Hungarian word *ház* is a Finno-Ugrian word (according to the linguists the similarity between it and the German *Haus* and the English *house* is purely coincidental and does not endorse an Indo-European kinship). In the current Finno-Ugrian the word *ház* is represented by *kat, kerku, kud, kota,* etc. Obviously these languages have drifted apart. "Accidental" consonances can occur by the dozen among various languages. For instance Hungarian *fogoly* (partridge) ≈ German *Vogel*, *eper* (strawberry) ≈ German *Erdbeere*, *ki* (who) ≈ French *qui*, *nyak* (neck) ≈ French *nuque*, *év* (year) ≈

97

Romanian *ev, nő* (woman) ≈ Chinese *nu*, *kér* (beg) ≈ Fidjian *kere*.

The linguists consider as the original source of a loan-word only the language from which it was directly taken. There are thus in Hungarian many words which are of Greek, Latin or Hebrew origin, but which arrived in Hungary via Germany or England. Consequently these words are considered to be German or English loan-words.

Early **Iranian loan-words** in the Hungarian language are: e.g.: *nemez* (felt), *tehén* (cow), *tej* (milk), and *tíz* (ten). From a never accurately identified ancient Turkic language, the Hungarian language has taken over: *harang* (bell), *nyak* (neck), *nyár* (summer), and *homlok* (fore-head).

Under the pressure of the tribes coming from the east (most directly the Sabirs), the Hungarian moved to the area of the Azov (Black) Sea. Here, the ancient Hungarians, the Finno-Ugrians and those becoming Finno-Ugrians living together, came into contact with Indo-Europeans (Persians), Altaian (Turks), and a number of Caucasian people who are very difficult to classify etymologically. Loan-words from the Persian which probably came from traders or other commercial contacts include: *vám* (duty), *vásár* (market), and *vár* (castle.) The Iranian-Alan loan-words included: *asszony* (woman), *híd* (bridge), and *vért* (armor).

Until the time of the conquest the most important influences affecting the Hungarians came from the Turks. These included the transfer of words and other cultural properties and - according to some researchers - even an intermingling and exchange of languages. From the period of the migrations the linguists identified about 300 ancient Turkish (Turkic) loan-words. (Péter Sára puts this number at 1,500.)

We will cite a number of linguistic proofs about the ancient **Turkish-Hungarian symbiosis,** grouped according to subject matter:

Body parts: *boka* (ankle), *gyomor* (stomach), *kar* (arm), *köldök* (navel), *szakáll* (beard).

Animal husbandry: *ártány* (hog), *bika* (bull), *borjú* (calf), *disznó* (pig), *kecske* (goat), *kos* (ram), *teve* (camel), *tyúk* (hen).

Agriculture: *alma* (apple), *borsó* (peas), *búza* (wheat), *eke* (plow), *gyümölcs* (fruit), *komló* (hops), *körte* (pear), *sarló* (sickle), *szérü* (barn), *tarló* (stubble).

Viniculture: *bor* (wine), *söprő* (lees), *szőlő* (grapes), *szűr* (filter).

Social life: *béke* (peace), *tanú* (witness), *tolmács* (interpreter), *törvény* (law), *bosszú* (vengeance), *bosszant* (annoy).

Religious life: *boszorkány* (witch), *bölcs* (wise), *ige* (the Word), *igéz* (conjures, casts a spell).

Dress: *bársony* (velvet), *csat* (clasp), *gyöngy* (pearl), *gyűrű* (ring), *köpönyeg* (cape), *tükör* (mirror).

Domiciles: *kapu* (door), *kút* (well), *sátor* (tent).

Furnishings: *bölcső* (cradle), *koporsó* (coffin), *söpör* (sweep), *szék* (chair).

Colors: *kék* (blue), *sárga* (yellow).

Some ancient eastern **Slavic** (ancient Russian and ancient Ukrainian) loan-words may have been taken up by the Hungarian language before the Conquest: *görög* (Greek), *lengyel* (Polish), *tanya* (farm).

In the ancient Hungarian period, the consonants *b, d, g, f, h* and *z* appeared in the Hungarian language and the velar *i* sound was converted to a palatal sound. It was also during this period that the grammatical structure developed, which is characteristic of the Hungarian language to this day. In the Indo-European languages the possessive is indicated by the use of possessive pronouns (*domus mea, mein Haus, ma maison,* my house). In Hungarian we

99

accomplish this by attaching a possessive suffix to the noun *(ház-am)*. These possessive suffixes evolved from the Finno-Ugrian personal pronouns which through use became firmly attached to the noun *(ház-én* ≈ house-I became *ház-am* ≈ house-my = my house).

There also evolved a third form of conjugation, the so-called *"ikes"* conjugation, which creates a passive-reflexive function in the singular form of certain verb tenses and forms: *tör - törik* (breaks, is being broken), *hall - hallik* (he hears, it can be heard), *ad - adatik* (give, is given), *mos - mosakodik* (wash, wash oneself).

One of the most interesting features of the Hungarian language, the system of verbal prefixes also probably started to develop about this time. It seems certain that *meg* (perfective), *el* (away), perhaps *ki (kivé-)* (out), *be (belé)* (into), *fel (fölé)* (over), and *le (lejé)* (down) appeared at the time of the ancient Hungarians. In some dialects, even today the verbal prefixes preserve something of their former independent existence: *haza-felé* (towards home), *padlás-belé* (into the attic).

The conjunctions, relative pronouns, and adverbs, which were already in use at the end of the ancient times, prove that there had to be subordinate clauses.

We can not speak of a single unified Hungarian language. At this time, the Hungarian language was still more a linguistic chain or a conglomerate of numerous dialects. These differences in the language may have been based on territorial or tribal divisions. (This is why there is much talk about tribal dialects.) The ancient dual linguistic forms which still exist in the Hungarian language and the linguistic "exceptions" suggest that in the ancient Hungarian period the language had to contain a variety of forms. According to one theory two dialects differed from each other by one using *s* and the other *sz* and traces of this distinction may be seen even today: *senyved* (lives under unfavorable circumstances) - *szenved* (suffers), *sövény* (hedge) - *sző* (knit). The ancient noun *jó* meaning river is seen only in the north-eastern part of the country and it may be assumed that it was familiar only to the tribes that settled in that area (*Sa-jó, Berek-jó,* in its modern form *Berettyó*).

What was the Hungarian language like and what did it sound like? Its phonetic system and scale were not as variable as they are today. Since the number of sounds were generated deep in the pharynx, the language was probably deeper and duller. Its vocabulary reflects both the equestrian-nomadic way of life and also the life after permanent settlements were established. Its derivational suffixes, its verbal and personal possessive suffixes and the rapid development of verbal prefixes made it possible to express delicate shades and nuances. The grammatical construction was characterized by terseness.

The inferences made about the Finno-Ugrian and Ugrian root languages indicate that they are far removed from the Hungarian language and that the kinship is obvious only to the experts. It was during the two thousand years of migration-settlement- and further migration that the "finished" Hungarian language evolved, which was used at the time of the conquest, which incorporated its most characteristic and peculiar features, which was close enough to the present Hungarian language to be at least partially recognizable and which determined the nature of the Hungarian language. The roots go back to the Finno-Ugrian, Ugrian original languages, but at the end of the conquest we are confronted with a brand new, different Hungarian language. Hence we view the period of the ancient Hungarians to be extremely important (and mysterious) from the point of view of the development of the Hungarian language and it seems likely that additional archaeological, historical, ethnographic and linguistic investigations will cast some light on this matter.

It must be considered a miracle that in such a conglomerate of languages, amongst an enormous number of ethnic and linguistic influences, incorporated into the

Turkic-speaking Kazar Empire, living in a symbiotic relationship with other languages and cultures, the Hungarian language was able to retain its Finno-Ugrian roots and develop into a quite specific, developed language. This process still hides a number of secrets and conundrums, since well-known, brilliant nations and languages (Kazar, Bulgarian-Turkish, Petcheneg and Cumanian) have disappeared without a trace along the same pathway.

From St. Stephen to King Mátyás.
The Golden Age of the Kingdom of Hungary and of Ancient Hungarian Culture

After their settlement, the conquering Hungarian tribes participated in campaigns throughout Europe. When the confederation of the tribes fell apart, the ruler, Géza, wished to integrate the country into the Christian-Feudal system of Europe. His son, (Saint) Stephen I, had himself crowned king in the year 1000, using the Holy Crown, which has since become the symbol of Hungarian state-hood. The foundation of the country is celebrated every August 20th, on the day of St. Stephen. King Stephen defeated powerful pagan chieftains, propagated Christian-ity, built a strong central power and organized the coun-ties and the dioceses. The feudal state was consolidated under his successors St. László I and Coloman Beauclerk II. A number of churches were built, first in the Roman style and then in the Gothic (Lébény, 1208, Ják, 1220). A number of them were erected on the foundations of old Christian basilicas, dating back to the Huns and the Avars.

In 1241 a new eastern nation, the Tatars (Altaian Mongolians) invaded Hungary. King Béla IV was unable to stop them in 1241 and was defeated in the battle of Muhi, near Miskolc. The Tatars destroyed half of the country and then very suddenly departed. On his return Béla IV encouraged the building of stone castles to serve as a defense against the Tatars. The House of Árpád died out in 1301 and the Anjou dynasty came into power. Lajos the Great, who from 1370 on was King of Poland as well, ruled an empire that extended from the Baltic to the Adriatic. From the end of the 14th century, Hungary was "Europe's Bastion" against the expansions of the Turks. The victory of János Hunyadi in 1456 at *Nándorfehérvár* (Belgrade) eliminated the Turkish threat for several decades. It is in memory of this victory that in all Christian lands of the world the church bells are rung at 12 noon. His son, the legendary King Mátyás (1458-1490) organized a strong army. He built a castle in Budapest and in Visegrád. This was the golden age of the Hungarian renaissance. While it lasted, the Hungarian people, its wealth, and its culture were equal in every way to any other country in Europe.

We consider the period between 1000 and 1526 A.D. as the golden age of the Kingdom of Hungary. During these years, from St. Stephen to King Mátyás, a unified country was created in East-Central-Europe which is without a parallel to this day and in which Slavs, Germans, and wandering Eastern peoples (Pechenegs, Cumanians and Jazygians) lived together in peace.

King Mátyás died in 1490, just two years before the discovery of America. Not much later an intensive Turkish attack began against Europe under the leadership of Suleiman. The Hungarians were defeated at Mohács in 1526 and shortly after that, the Turks occupied Buda. The 150 years of Turkish occupation had begun. The country was actually divided into three parts. The Habsburgs controlled the north and the west, the Turks were established in the central sections and in the east-southeast the Transylvanian Principality was established. The expansion of the Turks was held in check by the heroic defenders of the border fortresses. Kőszeg in 1532 defended Vienna and through Vienna, all of Europe, Temesvár and Eger were defended in 1552 and Szigetvár in 1566.

The Birth of Hungarian Writing.
Runes or Runic Script

The ancient writing of the Hungarians is runic. The origins of Hungarian (Turkic, Székely) runic writing are lost in antiquity. Its system differs from the system of the other European runic scripts. It can be classified with the Mesopotamian Sumerian and with Egyptian pictography. Its missing signs come from Phoenician sources, but some of the signs are reminiscent of the Etruscan runic characters. It seems therefore that the roots of Hungarian runic scripts go back to the highest cultures of ancient times.

The runic script is a notation of consonants in which the high and low vowels were indicated. They comprise phonetic symbols which may have one or more sound values and some of them may actually be symbols for a concept or for a picture. Since most of the runic documents came from Transylvania, it has been referred to as the Székely-Hungarian runic script.

A note by the Arabian Ibn Abu Jaqub an Nadim, made between 987-988, states that the Hungarians, called Turcs, made notations with a knife on arrows split in half. The only runic inscriptions that survived, however, were carved in stone or metal.

On the golden bowls of Nagyszentmiklós, originating from the 8th-9th centuries, Turkic and Hungarian runic inscriptions can be found. On the Avar bone needle holder from Szarvas and dating to the end of 8th century we also find Turkic and Hungarian runic inscriptions. The Hungarian version of the text is a magic one: *"Let this iron be against the demon Üngür. Let this needle pierce the demon, needle, needle sow up the evil one. Some you open up and some you stitch together. The demon Üngür shall not eat me, my God chase him away and devour him"*.

Number	Sound value	Sign	Number	Sound value	Sign
1.	a, á	◁ ◁ ᐱ	18.	m	ᛆ
2.	b	✕	19.	n	⟩
3.	c	↑	20.	ny	Ɗ
4.	cs	ᚺ	21.	o, ó	⟩
5.	d	✛	22.	ö, ő	⦶✕
6.	e, é	✗			Ⱪ⟨Z
7.	f	⊗	23.	p	∃ᘧ
8.	g	⋀	24.	r	Ⱨ Ⱨ Ⱨ
9.	gy	‡	25.	s	⋀
10.	h	⦼	26.	sz		
11.	h (ch)	ⱷ	27.	t	⅄
12.	i, í	✝	28.	ty	✗ ✗
13.	j	ᛏ	29.	u, ú	⋈ ⋈
14.	k	◆	30.	ü, ű	Ⴤ Ⴤ ⦻
15.	k (word ending)	ⱬ	31.	v	Ⅿ
16.	l	⋀	32.	z	ᚻ
17.	ly	⊙ ⊘	33.	zs	Ⴘ Ⴘ

Figure 5. The Székely alphabet (after Gyula Németh)

Additional important runic texts include: the Avar ring from Battonya with runic inscriptions, (8th century), the inscription in the brick of the Székelyderzs church (1531), the Nikolsburg runic alphabet in an incunabulum (1483), the carving in stone at the Homoródkarácsonfalva church (1495) and the runes and runic calendar from about 1690, found by Luigi Ferdinando Marsigli. The shards found in the Transylvanian Tordos and the three decorated clay tablets found in the Transylvanian Tatarlaka in 1961 are considered sensational finds. They contain symbols similar to the Sumerians and seem to refer to them.

We have preserved several runic manuscripts from the 16th century. These include the *Rudimenta* (Rudiments) of János Telegdi. The book written in Latin exists in several copies. One may be studied in the Hamburg library and the other in the Giessen Municipal library.

Before Christianity was widely disseminated, runic writing was probably more popular. It is mentioned by most of the early Hungarian grammarians. According to unconfirmed data, an attempt was made at the end of the 16th century, in Trencsén, to make the runic script the official script of the country. This may well have been the only such attempt to establish runic as the official script. Later the runic script was increasingly pushed back and became a form of secret writing and a curiosity among a select group. The word rune or runic is used in a variety of expressions which are very difficult to translate into English. They said he "had a lot of runes", when they meant that he had much to answer for, since originally debts were recorded in runic script on pieces of wood. There is a German parallel: *"er hat zu viel auf dem Kerbholz"* (he has too much on the scoring stick). Shepherds used runic sticks to record the number and condition of animals. The roster of the animals who died was known as the cadaver rune. As late as our century some runic symbols were still used, primarily in numbering, in animal husbandry and in identifying animals, trees, etc.

Hungarian Writing and the Roman Alphabet

The words *ró* (incising) and *rovás* (runic writing) are of Finno-Ugrian origin in the Hungarian language (they may have a Turkic origin). The Hungarian word *rovás* (runic writing) has spread by shepherding and partly by credit commerce into the German *(rawish, rosch)*, the Romanian *(ravás)*, the Slovakian *(rovás)* and the Polish *(rovasz)*. The words *írás* (writing) and *betű* (letter) have been present in the Hungarian language prior to the conquest and are of Turkic origin.

The gradual establishment of Hungarian writing, using Roman characters began in the 11th century, in the royal chancellery. With a number of modifications, this form of writing spread to a very wide circle by the beginning of the 16th century and is already quite close to the writing used today. It is readily understandable to a modern reader. Official orthography was born in 1832 when the Hungarian Scientific Academy accepted the responsibility for uniform regulations.

Runic writing was not suitable for recording lengthy texts and hence after the settlement and adaptation to European culture the use of Roman characters to record Hungarian texts started quite soon and spread widely during the succeeding centuries. If we discount the runic memorials, the Hungarian Roman character writing takes a prominent place in Europe. The Armenians have written records from the turn of the 4th and 5th centuries, the English from the 7th century the Germans from the 8th century and the Swedes from the 9th century.

Starting in the 11th century, Roman characters are used for Hungarian words inserted into foreign language texts (scatter-word texts). From the end of the 12th century, the Hungarian texts are continuous and unilingual and from the 14th century, we find entire Hungarian books written by hand. In the entire Uralian linguistic family, Hungarian has the earliest surviving texts.

Among the so-called scatter word texts we find Arabic, Persian, Byzantine, Greek and Latin texts into which Hungarian words had been inserted. The work of Constantinos Porphyrogenetos: On the Governance of the Empire, written in Greek in 950-951, contains about 50 words with Hungarian connotations (among them: *Etelköz, Álmos, Árpád, Tisza, Maros,* etc.).

The charter of the Veszprémvölgy convent was written in Greek before 1002. The document includes a number of important Hungarian words: *király* (king), *Veszprém* (the name of a city), *szántó* (plowing), *Szombat, Gerencsér, Palóznak* (place-names). The *Tihany Charter* was written in 1055. In this document we find the first fragmentary Hungarian sentence: *feheruuaru rea meneh hodu utu rea* (a [Székes] *Fehérvárra menő had[i] útra* - Onto the military road going to Fehérvár). This sentence is the very first and oldest linguistic record of the entire Uralian linguistic family. There are 58 Hungarian words in the document. It naturally includes Tihany (*Tichon*) since it is the charter of the monastery that is still active today. We also find the first mentions of Balaton (*Bolatin*), Siófok (*Fuk*) and Tolna (*Thelena*). The charter is preserved today in Pannonhalma in the Benedictine Monastery, but a copy can be found in the Tihany Monastery on the shores of Lake Balaton. The scatter word records are followed by handwritten texts. There are four smaller Hungarian written records dating back to before 1350.

The first consistent Hungarian textual record, the *Funerary Oration and Prayer* dates from 1192-1195 and was found in the so-called *Pray Codex.* It was written somewhere in Transdanubia.

The *Funeral Oration* is a 32 line valedictory. The text is written with a fairly primitive spelling, but at that time each character may have had more than one tonal value.

The linguists were nevertheless able to reconstruct the contemporary pronunciation. Thus we have a reasonably accurate idea about the way they talked in Hungary at the end of the 12th century.

The *Funerary Oration* begins thus: *"Behold, my flock, with thine eyes what we are. Behold, we are dust and ashes. With how much Divine grace has [God] created Adam our father and gave [him] Paradise as a dwelling place. And He told him, that he may eat all the fruit in Paradise and forbade him to eat only a single fruit, but He told him why he should not eat of that fruit. Behold, on the day that you eat of that fruit you will die the death of deaths. He heard from the Creator God that he would die, but he forgot about it…"*

> *"Látjátok feleim, szemetekkel, mik vagyunk?*
> *Íme, por és hamu vagyunk. Mennyi malaszttal*
> *ellátva teremtette [isten] a mi atyánkat,*
> *Ádámot, és a Paradicsomot adta [neki]*
> *lakóhelyül. És azt mondta neki, hogy a*
> *Paradicsomban való minden gyümölccsel*
> *éljen, csupán egy fa gyümölcsétől tiltotta el őt,*
> *de megmondta neki, mért ne egyék belőle. Íme,*
> *amely napon eszel e gyümölcsből, halálnak*
> *halálával halsz. Hallotta a teremtő istentől,*
> *hogy meg fog halni, de megfeledkezett róla…"*

The *Königsberg fragment* was written presumably at the beginning of the 13th century. The codex was torn apart by a bookbinder of Wrocłav, since it contained material that he did not understand. He used the strips of paper in the bindings of other books. In the surviving textual record we find a eulogy of Mary's virginity and religious stories. It begins: "From the beginning of the world something like this has never happened [to us], that a virgin girl should give birth to a son and keep the mirror of her virginity unspotted and that we should know nothing about this. We know her and see her as a virgin girl, who holds a miraculous son in her lap, whom she bathes, washes, feeds and suckles just like a mother its newborn."

The so-called *Gyulafehérvár Lines* were created in 1260-1270. The text of 15 lines on Jesus sounds like a poem. In modern language:

> Önnön tanítványának árulása.
> A saját nemzetbeli népének vádaskodása.
> Jeruzsálem városának megtisztelő fogadása.
> Isten fiának ártatlansága.
> Halálának szidalmas kínja.
> Boldogasszonynak szeme láttára.

And in English:
> The treason of his own disciple.
> The accusations of his own people.
> The honorable reception in Jerusalem.
> The innocence of the Son of God.
> The degrading torture of his death.
> Under the eyes of the Blessed Virgin Mary.

The first true poem in the Hungarian language, the *Ancient Hungarian Lamentation of Mary,* was created around 1300. It was found in a codex entitled *Sermones*, in 1922 in Belgium in Leuven. It survived the torching of the library in 1940. In exchange for some Netherlandic codices, Belgium returned this codex to Hungary in 1982. The *Ancient Hungarian Lamentation of Mary* is a masterful translation of a Latin poem in which the Virgin Mary laments her crucified Son with the eternal pain of all mothers who must bury their sons:

> Világ világa, virágnak virága,
> Keserűen kínzatol, vas szegekkel veretel.

And in English:
> *Light of the world, flower of flowers,*
> *You are bitterly tortured, transfixed with nails of iron.*

There are various lists of words (glossaries) which show the language of daily life. *János of Rotenburg* gives a list of useful words and sentences in German and Latin translation, compiled in 1422:

Ennek mi neve?	What is this called?
Melyik az igaz út Budára?	Which is the real way to Buda?
Honnét jössz?	Where do you come from?
Hová mész?	Where are you going?
Asszony mossad ingemet!	Woman, wash my shirt!
Végy te nekem egy sarut!	You, buy me some sandals!
Vagyon-e bor?	Is there any wine?
Szakács, adj te húst!	Cook, give me meat!

The oldest memorial of popular healing incantations (related to Christ) are in the 1488 *Bagonya Incantation*. The oldest Hungarian popular poetic fragment is the so-called *Sopron Flower Song,* a ballad from 1490. We show it in the original and also in a modern Hungarian version:

> *Wyrag, th/u/dyad, theuled el kel mennem.*
> *Es the yrethed kel gyazba ewlteznem.*

In modern Hungarian spelling:
> *Virág, tudjad, tőled el kell mennem.*
> *És te íretted kell gyászba öltöznem.*

And in English: *Flower, know that I must leave you, / It is for you I have to dress in mourning.*

The first really juicy Hungarian curse is found in the *Dubnicz Chronicle* of 1497.

The smaller documents were followed by manuscript books and codices. Mátyás Hunyadi, at the peak of Hungarian royal power in the second half of the 15th century, had a library estimated to contain 500-1000 volumes. These books were referred to as Corvina, from the Hunyadi heraldic animal the raven *(corvus)*. Corvina codices were favorite presents among kings and many fell victim to the destructive wars of the next centuries. We have only 46 volumes today. (Many of these can be found in the Budapest University Library.)

The oldest continuous text, written only in Hungarian, is the original of the *Jókai Codex,* which must have been written between 1372 and 1400. The surviving copy is from 1448. It deals with the life and legends of St. Francis, in a very enjoyable style. It contains the story of the "converted wolf" whom St. Francis convinces not to attack people any more. It also includes the sermon to the birds and the story about the doubting brother secretly erasing the holy stigmata on the Christ mural, upon which the wounds started to bleed all over again.

The book was probably used in a Franciscan monastery and was sent north to safeguard it from the Turks. A student in Nyitra came across it accidentally in 1851 when he was throwing a bunch of books about. Later owners put it into an auction in London and the Hungarian government was fortunate to purchase it for 1450 English pounds. The first codex written entirely in Hungarian was returned to the mother country in 1925 and was called after the greatest Hungarian novelist, the Jókai Codex.

The first Hungarian biblical translations were performed in the Czech Hussite spirit at the beginning of the 15th century. We have only copies, produced between 1450 and 1500. The priests Tamás and Bálint follow the Czech accented orthography. The so-called *Hussite Bible* actually consists of three codices, the Viennese, the Munich and the Apor codices.

The first Hungarian version of the *Lord's Prayer* is found in the *Munich Codex* of 1466.

During the reign of Mátyás, András Hess established a

printing press in Buda in 1471. The first, partly Hungarian, printed work was published in Cracow in 1527. Thus the history of the Hungarian language from the 10th to the 16th century can be followed on the basis of written material.

The *Tihany Charter* (1055) still contains certain words which show the alleged Finno-Ugrian terminal vowels:

Original	Later form	Modern usage	English
hodu	*hod*	*had*	*army*
utu	*ut*	*út*	*road*

In later usage these terminal vowels were lost.

A principal trend was an opening of the vowels during which evolution *u* became *o, o* became *a, ü* became *ö, i* became *e*: *fuk - fok* (degree), *mogos - magas* (high), *kükén - kökény* (blackthorn), and *higy - hegy* (mountain).

Three syllable words were shortened to two syllables so that in the majority of cases the vowel of the first syllable was lengthened and the vowel of the second syllable was dropped: *malina - málna* (raspberry), and *palica - pálca* (rod).

Suffixes (*-ból, -ből* from the noun *bél*), postpositions (*után* [after], *együtt* [together], *között* [amid], *gyanánt* [by way of]), verbal prefixes (*alá* [under], *egybe* [into one], *össze* [together], *vissza* [back], *körül* [around], *hozzá* [to], and *neki* [get into, see to]) were born in this period.

We can observe a simplification of conjugation and the elimination of certain tenses in other languages as well. In the ancient Hungarian written language there was a passive (*"ikes"*) conjugation which has almost completely disappeared.

The vocabulary is generally enlarged by existing words being given a new meaning or new meanings. Even before accepting Christianity, the Hungarians were familiar with the words *isten* (God), *lélek* (soul), and *ördög* (devil). Their meaning was later adapted to Christian usage. The word *úr* originally meant royal prince. Later the highest nobles were known as *főúr*. Today everybody is an *úr*. *Kovács úr* (Mr. Kovács), *Miniszter úr* (Mr. Minister), and even *tolvaj úr* (Mr. thief - jocular).

Loan-Words in the Hungarian Language

The linguists have thoroughly explored the contacts of the words in the common language and in the dialects with other languages. In the light of these studies, it appears that the Hungarian language has taken part and is taking part in a multilateral cultural exchange in the Carpathian Basin, between north and south and between east and west. In these exchange contacts, the Hungarian language has taken over a large number of words, but has always adjusted them to its own linguistic system and was thus able to preserve its own individuality.

In the Carpathian Basin, the Hungarians came under the influence of three major languages: Slavic, German and Latin. We may also mention Byzantine, Greek, Italian, French, Romanian and finally, Ottoman-Turk influences. Mention must also be made of the languages of the Petchenegs, Cumanians and Jazygians which were absorbed by Hungarian during the Middle Ages.

The linguistic contacts with the Slavs seem to be the strongest ones. There are several reasons for this. The Hungarians had encountered the Slavs already at the time of the migrations and in the Carpathian Basin there were Slavic settlements (at that time still not sharply demarcated Bulgarians, southern Slavs, northern Slavs and Moravians). Place names of Slavic origin survive to this day: *Tapolca* (in Trasndanubia and next to Miskolc), *[Nagy]kanizsa, Balaton, Visegrád,* etc.

The lake we call Balaton today was called Pelso by the Pannonian Illyrians (and Indo-European people of the Roman Empire). The term *Pelso* has survived from Roman times in several locations. The name *Balaton* is derived from a Slavic word meaning swamp or mud. The German name for the lake, *Plattensee*, may have a similar

116

etymology. The similarity of the form and meaning of the Slavic and Illyrian words is striking.

The word *Visegrád* is present in most Slavic languages and its original meaning is: a castle on a hill within a city. In the Visegrád in Hungary, the Romans established a military camp in the bend of the Danube. When the country was established, it was here that the first castle was erected. In 1335 the Polish, Czech and Hungarian Kings reached an economic and political cooperative agreement at the "congress" of Visegrád. In his castle in Visegrád, on the banks of the Danube, King Mátyás maintained one of Europe's most magnificent courts.

Slavic loan-words appeared in many administrative, economic, religious and everyday contexts, between the conquest and the lost battle of Mohács. The linguist István Kniezsa puts their number at 1252 (484 in the common language, 694 in the vernacular and 74 archaic). Some of the most important groups are:

Church and religion: *keresztény* (Christian), *pap* (priest), *barát* (brother), *apát* (Abbot), *apáca* (nun), *csoda* (miracle), *vecsernye* (vespers), *zsolozsma* (chant), *karácsony* (Christmas).

Days: *szerda* (Wednesday), *csütörtök* (Thursday), *péntek* (Friday). *Hétfő* (Monday), and *vasárnap* (Sunday) are Hungarian composite words. *Kedd* (Tuesday) is derived from the Hungarian *kettő* (two), while *szombat* (Saturday) came to Hungarian from the original Hebrew via the Slavs.

Administrative and legal life: *király* (king), *nádorispán* (palatine), *tiszt* (officer), *szolga* (servant), *megye* (county), *pecsét* (seal), *tömlöc* (jail), *kaloda* (pillory), *poroszló* (bailiff), *pénz* (money), *zálog* (pawn).

Agriculture: *csoroszlya* (coulter of a plow), *gerendely* (plow beam), *borona* (harrow), *kasza* (scythe), *villa* (fork), *kalapács* (hammer), *barázda* (furrow), *parlag* (fallow land), *ugar* (fallow land), *gabona* (grain), *rozs* (rye), *zab* (oats), *szalma* (straw), *korpa* (bran), *bab* (bean), *cékla* (beets), *dinnye* (melon), *kapor* (dill), *káposzta* (cabbage), *lencse* (lentil), *mák* (poppy seed), *répa* (carrot), *retek* (radish), *uborka* (pickle), *barack* (peach), *cseresznye* (cherry), *szilva* (plum).

Animal husbandry: *bárány* (lamb), *birka* (sheep), *bivaly* (buffalo), *kanca* (mare), *kakas* (rooster), *galamb* (pigeon), *macska* (cat), *csorda* (herd), *akol* (corral), *jászol* (manger), *ketrec* (cage), *iga* (yoke), *járom* (harness), *patkó* (horse-shoe), *széna* (hay), *kazal* (hayrack), *pásztor* (shepherd).

Manufacture and trade: *bodnár* (cooper), *esztergályos* (lathe operator), *kocsma* (tavern), *kocsmáros* (tavern keeper), *kovács* (smith), *mészáros* (butcher), *molnár* (miller), *takács* (weaver), *guzsaly* (distaff), *korong* (disc), *abroncs* (hoop), and *kád* (tub).

Shipping: *kormány* (tiller), *vitorla* (sail), and *csónak* (boat).

Military: *kopja* (halberd), *parittya* (slingshot), *puzdra* (quiver), *számszeríj* (crossbow), *zászló* (flag), and *vitéz* (soldier).

Family: *cseléd* (servant), *család* (family), *dédunoka* (great grandchild), *koma* (godfather), *dajka* (wet nurse).

House, home: *ablak*, (window), *gerenda* (rafter), *kemence* (stove), *oszlop* (column), *konyha* (kitchen), *pince* (cellar), *pitvar* (yard), *pad* (bench), *asztal* (table), *abrosz* (table cloth), *polc* (shelf), *párna* (pillow), *dunna* (comforter), *pokróc* (blanket), *kas* (hive), *kosár* (basket).

Eating: *ebéd* (lunch), *vacsora* (dinner), *csésze* (cup), *palack* (flask), *kása* (millet), *kalács* (cake), *pogácsa* (small lard cake), and *zsír* (fat).

Clothing: *ruha* (dress), *csuha* (monk's habit), *nadrág*

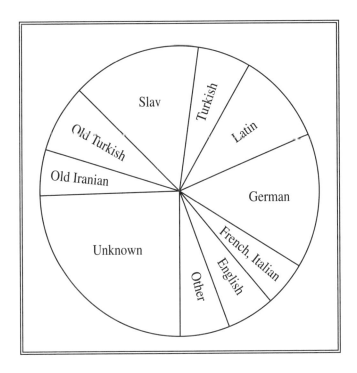

Figure 6. Groups of loan-words in the Hungarian language (the ratios reflect the contents of the Historical-Etymological Dictionary)

(pants), *palást* (cape), *szoknya* (skirt), *borotva* (razor), *szappan* (soap).

Nations: *bolgár* (Bulgarian), *bosnyák* (Bosnian), *cseh* (Czech), *görög* (Greek), *horvát* (Croatian), *német* (German), *oláh* (Wallachian), *olasz* (Italian), *szász* (Saxonian), *zsidó* (Jewish).

Nature: *barlang* (cave), *szikla* (rock), *mocsár* (swamp), *iszap* (mud).

Plants: *borostyán* (ivy), *gomba* (mushroom), *lapu* (plantain), *moha* (moss), *pázsit* (lawn), *csipke* (lace), and *bodza* (elder).

Animals: *hörcsög* (hamster), *medve* (bear), *patkány* (rat), *vidra* (otter), *szarka* (magpie), and *veréb* (sparrow).

Adjectives: *buja* (lush), *drága* (expensive), *csorba* (dull) *derék* (worthy), *gonosz* (evil), *goromba* (rude), *görbe* (bent), etc.

The numerous Slavic-Hungarian word associations have led some time ago to the assumption that the Hungarians arrived in the Carpathian Basin as a purely nomadic people and took over all concepts dealing with settlement and with establishing a country from the Slavs whom they found here. Today this view is untenable. According to archaeological and historical evidence the ancient Hungarians had led a settled form of life for several hundreds of years, cultivated land, had artisans and engaged in commerce in addition to their warlike activities. It seems extremely unlikely that they would have been unfamiliar with the words considered Slavic loanwords, like *pénz* (money), *király* (king), *számszeríj* (crossbow), *patkó* (horse-shoe), *járom* (yoke), *abrak* (fodder), *széna* (hay), *pányva* (rope), or the adjective *drága* (expensive). Perhaps they used different words for these concepts? Maybe they did a certain, limited "wordswap" in the Carpathian Basin and "exchanged" these basic concepts for Slavik words?

The large number of root-word concurrences suggest that the ancient Slavs may have lived together with the ancient Hungarians or proto-Hungarians (e.g. white Ogurs or Avars), and that their languages had manifold concurrences. Later on, the jointly evolved, simpler Slavic words were taken over by the Hungarians. It is a known phenomenon that a word for a known concept or item is changed by the language for another word. If this happens on a very large scale, we are seeing an exchange of languages. This is clearly not applicable to the Hungarians and the Slavs. It is also possible that assuming the presence of such a very large number of Slavic loan-words in Hungarian is an exaggeration and that the loan-words moved in the opposite direction. Among the examples of loan-words listed and believed to be of Slavic origin, we can find numerous Hungarian word roots: *ded/déd/did, kis-ded* (infant), *déd-mama* (great grand mother), *did-ereg* (shivers), and even *kerek-ded* (rounded). The latter example also sheds some light on the peculiar linguistic manipulation of loan-word increases. According to the etymological dictionary of the Hungarian language, the word *család* (family) is a loan-word of Slavic origin. Later on and obviously within the Hungarian language the word *cseléd* (servant) evolved from *család*, according to a regular tonal and interpretational parallelism characteristic of ancient Hungarian. Yet this new word, created in Hungarian and non-existing in Slavic is still considered to be of "Slavic origin" by the dictionary.

The word *karácsony* (Christmas) is also presumably derived from the Slavic (southern Slav, possible Slovakian), and is allegedly traced back to an ancient Slav root. (We obviously cannot talk about Slovakian in an 11th-13th century context.) András Tardy suggested that *kara* and *cson* may be Turkic and Mongolian in origin meaning black wolf. The word karácsony does appear in several Hungarian place names, such as Karácsond and Karácsonyfalva and derivatives can be found dating to the 11th to 14th centuries. It is also of interest that other than the ordinary meaning of black wolf, it also referred to the winter solstice among some Asiatic people, meaning the darkest day of the year.

Much less interest was shown by the linguists in the effects of the Hungarian language on the Slavic languages. Ferenc Gregor, shows in one of his papers that by the end of the 18th century about 600 Hungarian loan-words have appeared in the Slovakian language. These include *buzogány* (mace), *csákány* (battle axe), *dárda* (lance), *fegyveres* (armed), *hadnagy* (lieutenant), *janicsár* (janissary), *labda* (ball), *mozsár* (mortar), and *szerszám* (tool). According to István Nyomárkay, there are about 1,000 Hungarian words that have been assimilated for some time into the Serbian and Croatian languages. Some examples: *vármegye* (county), *város* (city), *főszolgabíró* (lord lieutenant), *drótos* (wired), *inas* (male servant), *bekecs* (mackinaw), *bunda* (fur), *dolmány* (pelisse), and *kabát* (coat). Even more peculiar are some Hungarian words which were formally considered to be of Slavic origin, but which were modified in the Hungarian language and were returned to one of the Slavic languages in this altered form. E.g.: *akó* (a measure of capacity), *asztal* (table), *csárda* (tavern), *gazda* (farmer) *kormány* (government), *parlag* (fallow), *sánta* (lame), *mészáros* (butcher), and *vajda* (voivode).

The appearance of **German loan-words** is dated to the time of the establishment of the Hungarian Kingdom. This may mean only the presence of documentary evidence. The Hungarians were probably in contact with Germanic tribes at an earlier time, for instance in the Avar Empire and during some of their campaigns. The presumptive ancient high German or perhaps very early Bavarian loan-words are the remnants of such contacts (e.g.: *sarabol* [hoe], *püspök* [bishop], and *pünkösd* [Pentecost]).

The wife of St. Stephen, Gisella was Bavarian. On her invitation missionary priests and knights appeared in the country. They were followed by settlers. The Germans arriving in medieval times played a major role in the creation of an urban bourgeoisie, and of a system of guilds. They were also very active in the mining industry. It was under these conditions that loan-words flourished. In the cities the major role was played by Bavarian-Austrian settlers, while the Szepes and Transylvanian settlers brought

122

with them the dialect of mid-Germany and the Rhine-Mosel area.

After the Turks were ejected, numerous Germans settled in Hungary. German was the generally used conversational medium in the Hungarian cities. According to some recollections, 200 years ago more German than Hungarian words could be heard in the streets of Buda and of Pest. A few of the more important groups of German loan-words:

Court life: *hopmester* (court official), *herceg* (prince), *gróf* (count), *porkoláb* (jailer), *ostrom* (siege), *zsákmány* (plunder), *kastély* (castle), *torony* (tower), *párkány* (ledge), *erkély* (balcony), *tánc* (dance), and *lator* (rogue, woman chaser).

Dressing: *gallér* (collar), *párta* (headdress), *gyolcs* (linen), *pendely* (shirt), *prém* (fur), and *gyémánt* (diamond).

Holidays: *farsang* (carnival), *tornir* (tourney), *hazárd* (gambling).

City, guild, industry: *polgár* (bourgeois), *polgármester* (mayor), *cégér* (signboard), *céh* (guild), *kontár* (counter), *borbély* (barber), *erszény* (purse), *persely* (money box), *fertály* (quarter), *meszely* (old liquid measure), *font* (pound), *krajcár* (penny), *fillér* (penny), *garas* (farthing), *kohó* (smelting furnace), *érc* (metal).

Rural life: *csűr* (barn), *kaptár* (beehive), *major* (farm), *puttony* (butt), *komp* (ferry), *istráng* (rope), *trágár* (foul-mouthed). (This last meaning is relatively recent. In earlier times it meant wandering salesmen and even roaming minstrels.)

According to the researches of Károly Mollay, 526 German loan-words had entered the Hungarian language by the end of the 16th century.

Latin was the connecting language between European cultures. It came to the region of the Danube first when this area was part of the Roman Empire and then again, after 970, when the Roman version of Christianity was introduced. There were about 500 years between these two periods, but records show that there was some continued transmission of Latin in Pannonia (e.g.: the Illyrians).

Latin had a dominant role in Hungarian governmental, economic and cultural life. Until the middle of the 19th century, Latin was the lingua franca of Europe, including the polyglot Kingdom of Hungary and was used in both personal and official communication. The earliest charters, laws, chronicles and literature in Hungary were written in Latin. In the oldest Hungarian library list, the records of the Benedictine Abbey of Pannonhalma of 1083, the well-known Latin grammar of Donatus is listed. The first really significant Hungarian poet, Janus Pannonius, wrote his poems in Latin in the 15th century. Latin was the language of the Church, of science and of the schools. The first Hungarian grammar was written in Latin and modeled on the Latin grammar (János Sylvester, 1539). Hungarian became the official language of the country only in 1844. Until 1948 the teaching of Latin in Hungarian high schools was a universal practice. The first Hungarian texts are Hungarian codices which are mostly translated from the Latin and hence are filled with Latinisms, quite foreign to the spoken language. Such Latinisms include passive constructions, the use of past tenses and improperly employed infinitives. In medieval Hungary a peculiar Latin dialect developed that was known as Hungarian Latin. In this dialect the *h* was unaspirated, the *s* was pronounced like an *sh* or a *zs*, and the *g* before an *e* or *i* was pronounced as a *dz* or *gy*. (It may be due to this medieval practice, that the Hungarian "s" is still pronounced as *sh* and *g+y* is pronounced as *gy*).

Comenius, the eminent educator, who lived in Hungary in the 17th century, chastised the Hungarians for their faulty Latin pronunciation. In the works of the 19th century Hungarian writers we find an enormous number of German and Latin quotations and words. For them and for their readers this multilingual education was a matter of course. This is no longer true today and some of the works of our classic authors have to be published with extensive notes and glossaries. E.g.: The new, 100 volume edition of the novels of Mór Jókai had to be accompanied by a two volume *Jókai dictionary* that contains about 23,000 entries, including some with more than one meaning. These entries illustrate and explain Jókai's use of Latin, German, French, Italian, English, Spanish, Russian, Polish, Slovakian, Romanian, Greek, Turkish, Arabic, Hebrew words, as well as words from regional dialects and archaic Hungarian words. Some of the more important words of Latin origin in Hungarian are:

Church: *templom* (church), *kápolna* (chapel), *monostor* (monastery), *klastrom* (cloister), *sekrestye* (sacristy), *eklézsia* (parish), *oltár* (altar), *orgona* (organ), *ostya* (host), *próféta* (prophet), *mártír* (martyr), *kanonok* (canon), *prépost* (presbyter), *paradicsom* (paradise), *purgatórium* (purgatory).

School: *iskola* (school), *kollégium* (college), *professzor* (professor), *tábla* (black-board), *kréta* (chalk), *spongya* (sponge), *papíros* (paper), *szekunda* (bad mark), *vakáció* (vacation), *diktál* (dictates).

Plants: *akác* (locust), *cédrus* (cedar), *pálma* (palm), *citrom* (lemon), *majoránna* (marjoram), *petrezselyem* (parsley), *ibolya* (violet).

Animals: *elefánt* (elephant), *tigris* (tiger), *párduc* (leopard), *hiéna* (hyena), *krokodilus* (crocodile), *vipera* (viper), *páva* (peacock), and *fülemüle* (nightingale).

Medicine: *patika* (pharmacy), *pirula* (pill), *diéta* (diet), *kúra* (cure), *pestis* (plague).

Administration and law: *notárius* (notary), *fiskális* (attorney - shyster), *prókátor* (lawyer), *lajstrom* (register), *voks* (vote), *paktum* (contract).

House: *kúria* (country house), *porta* (house, home), *kamra* (chamber), *grádics* (staircase), *pádimentum* (ground floor), *tégla* (brick), *almárium* (wardrobe).

Months: *január* (January), *február* (February), *március* (March), etc.

The number of commonly used Latin words in Hungarian books exceeds 200, although in professional textbooks this number may be substantially larger.

In the 11th and 12th centuries strong contacts continued between Hungary and Byzantium. **Byzantine Greek words** in Hungarian include: *paplan* (comforter), *iszák* (knapsack), *katona* (soldier), *paripa* (steed), *szamár* (donkey), and *tímár* (tanner).

The first **Italian loan-words** appear in the 12th century. The Hungarians were particularly prone to take over the names of the products peddled by Italian merchants: *füge* (fig), *narancs* (orange), *mandula* (almond), *datolya* (date), and *rizs* (rice). Some of the technical maritime terms also come from the Italian: *sajka* (small boat), *gálya* (galley), *bárka* (barque, later referring to the Venetian gondola). Urban words: *piac* (market) and *kandalló* (fireplace), entertainment: *trombita* (trumpet), *tréfa* (jest), *csúf* (ugly, but originally meaning a clown). Others: *csepű* (oakum), *pálya* (course, path). The prize for winners of a race: *köntös* (cloak), *zászló* (flag).

The name of the town Firenze was used in the designation of numerous currencies, e.g.: the English florin and the Hungarian *forint*. The Florentines first minted coins with flowers on them in 1252. The first forints in Hungary were minted after the extinction of the Árpád family, under the Anjou Charles Robert in 1335. The Hungarian coinage is again called forint since 1946.

Hungary also has a *Velence* which may refer to early Italian settlers. A shallow lake between Budapest and Lake Balaton may have received the name Velence from a settlement adjacent to it. The word is etymologically probably identical with Venetia.

The Hungarians call the Italians *olasz*, and there are a number of communities in Hungary which contain this word: e.g.: Olasz, Olaszfa, Olaszfalu, Olaszliszka, Bodrogolaszi, etc. These communities were settled by Italians, or perhaps, by Walloons.

In the 11th century the Hungarian ruling house became related to the French ruling house and consequently French nobles, knights and later friars came to Hungary. In some cities, the German settlers were joined by Walloon settlers and we know of about a dozen early **French loan-words**: *dézsma* (tithe), *lakat* (lock), *kilincs* (door handle), *szekrény* (cupboard), *mécs* (wick), *tárgy* (object), *zománc* (enamel), *korc* (hem), *furmint* (a type of wine), and *paraj* (spinach). In the Tokaj-Hegyalja wine growing region there are several communities incorporating the word *tállya* (Andornaktálya, Nagytálya, etc.) which is probably of ancient French or Walloon origin, meaning clearing. It may also come from the Italian *telie,* meaning valley.

Hungarian-Romanian contacts date back to the 12th century. The number of early **Romanian loan-words** is small. The first written Romanian loan-word appears only in the 14th century: *ficsúr* (dandy). Approximately a dozen Romanian words have been taken over into the language: *cimbora* (pal), *mokány* (spunky), *fustély* (cudgel), *áfonya* (huckleberry), *tokány* (stew), *málé* (polenta), and *kaláka* (co-op work, bee). In the Mezőség and in Transylvanian Hungarian several hundred Romanian words have appeared, particularly during the last century, and a large number of Hungarian words have gone over into the Romanian language: *ország* (country), *város* (city), *vármegye* (county), *tábor* (camp), *sereg* (army), and *vám* (cusoms duty).

The Magyarized Eastern Peoples (Petchenegs, Cumanians, Jazygians) and Their Linguistic Remnants

After the 896 Conquest, the Hungarian kings accepted and settled smaller eastern, Altaic-Turkic (Petcheneg, Uz and Cumanian) and Iranian (Alani and Jazygian) tribes.

The Petchenegs were formerly at war with the Hungarians, but from the second half of the 11th century they asked for permission to settle in the Carpathian Basin and this request was granted by the Hungarian kings. Their language is lost and no consistent linguistic memorials survive. Place names suggest that they were Turks of the Kipchak family. Their memory is preserved in Hungary by placenames like *Besenyő, Besnyő, Beseny,* etc. (There are people in Hungary who are very proud of their Petcheneg heritage.)

In the 13th century, the Hungarian kings permitted the Cumanians to settle in the middle part of the country. Today regional designations, like *Kiskunság* and *Nagykunság* as well as a number of city names, *Kiskunfélegyháza, Kunszentmárton,* etc., preserve their memory. Words of Cumanian origin include: *csődör* (stallion), *komondor* (a breed of dog), *kun* (Cumanian), *orosz* (Russian), *csősz* (guardian), *kalauz* (conductor), *koboz* (lute), and perhaps also *balta* (ax), *csákány* (pickaxe), *bicsak* (knife), *örmény* (Armenian), and *kobak* (pate). The Cumanians have lost their language but they have preserved their identity to this day. We are familiar with their language from the 1303 *Codex Cumanus,* which was discovered in Venice. In the first half of the 20th century an attempt was made in Hungary to revive the Cumanian language. The text of the *Lord's Prayer* was reconstructed in Cumanian and taught to children in the Kunság. It is thus possible that some of the older people of that region still know one or two Cumanian words. The world famous linguist and researcher of the Cumanians is the Hungarian István Mándoky-Kongur.

The Cumanians and the Jazygyans were frequently handled together. (At one time there was even a joint Jazygian-Cumanian adminsitrative area.) The Jazygians and the Cumanians probably arrived at about the same time. In exchange for their military service, they were directly accountable to the king only. It appears that the Jazygians were a group of Alanai speaking an Iranian language. They engaged in agriculture in the area between the Zagyva and the Tarna and asked the king for the area which later was known as the Jászság, while the more mobile Cumanians settled on the Alföld plains better suited for animal husbandry. A Jazygian word list from 1442 is preserved, e.g.: *soseg izon* – Good morning!; *kheevef* (bread), *kasa* (millet), *dan* (water), *karak* (chicken), etc.

By the 16th century the linguistic exchange was complete and in the Hungarian language no Jazygian words are preserved, other than some place names (*Jászberény, Jászárokszállás, Jászszentlászló,* as well as *eszlár, oszlár,* etc.). There still is a Jazygian identity even today, people refer to their Jazygian origins and in the museum in Jászberény, they are guarding the ancient symbol of the Jazygians, the Lehel- or Jazygyan horn, which takes us back directly to the horn cult of the Caucasian tribes. In 1754 the Jazygo-Cumanians bought back their rights for self-administration (Jazygo-Cumanian redemption) which they were able to maintain until 1876.

The fate of the Petchenegs, Cumanians and Jazygians is similar in many ways to that of the Hungarians. They came from the east, divided into several groups and were in contact with numerous tribes and languages. Their settlement in Hungary and their change in language may be a feature of their affinity for the Hungarian way of life and for Hungarian mentality. The fact that they kept their identity shows that language and identity are not necessarily inseparable.

From the Turkish Occupation to the Reorganization of the Country

After the loss of the battle of Mohács in 1526, the central parts of the country were occupied by the Turks for a century and a half. In the Alföld, most of the population moved into the cities, but major parts of the country became depopulated. There are some buildings that recall the Turkish occupation: minarets, turbeks (funerary chapels), and steam baths. There are also approximately 30 **Ottoman-Turkish loan-words:**

Eating: *ibrik* (mug), *findzsa* (pot), *pite* (fruit pie), *tepsi* (frying pan).

Clothing: *zseb* (pocket), *kalpag* (headgear), *pamut* (wool), *papucs* (slipper), *mamusz* (felt slippers).

Weapons: *dzsida* (lance), *handzsár* (sword), *korbács* (whip), *kancsuka* (knout). (This last word is used even today by shepherds and riders in the areas formerly occupied by the Turks.)

Useful items: *kefe* (brush), *dívány* (davenport), *burnót* (snuff), *csibuk* (pipe).

It is at this time that the relatively rare *dzs,* e.g.: *handzsár*, enters the Hungarian language. The memory of the Turks is kept alive also by many words which are not of Turkish origin but which incorporate the word *török* (Turkish) into another word: *törökbors* (paprika), *törökbúza* (corn), *török kávé* (Turkish coffee - a relatively weak, boiled coffee, vastly different from the poisonously strong *"presszó"* coffee favored by the Hungarians today), *törökméz* (Turkish delight), *törökparadicsom* (eggplant), and also by a number of place names such as *Törökszentmiklós, Törökbálint, Törökkoppány,* etc.

In the cities along the rivers (in Mohács, Baja, Ráckeve, Buda and Pest), Serbs and other southern Slavs, fleeing from the Turks, settled about this time. They kept their religion, language and customs to this day. The Mohács processional is a major spectacle and performance at the time of the carnival. The *busók (busuk)* (processioners) wearing wooden fright masks and making hideous noises attack the Turkish tents set up in the main square. The custom is explained by claiming that it was these masked, noisy *busók* (processioners) who liberated Mohács from the Turks (in 1686). After the expulsion of the Turks, the Hungarian Kingdom became part of the Habsburg Empire. The resettlement of the depopulated parts was started, partly by internal migrations. A group of the Palóc living in the north moved to the southern part of the Alföld. We refer to this as "Palóc swarming". They maintain their peculiar dialect in the new location until this day. In addition, there were also German and Slovakian settlements.

The awakening of the Hungarian national culture and language started during the period of Enlightenment, beginning in 1772 and continued during the Reform Period during the early years of the 19th century. The struggles for reforms led to rebellion and to the war of independence against the Habsburg Empire. After a bitter period of reconstruction, the "Compromise" of 1867 led to the establishment of the Austro-Hungarian Monarchy. A strong German influence became manifest in the language as well and this influence actually began at the beginning of the 18th century. While the earlier German loan-words were fully assimilated into the language, the new **German loan-words** were readily recognizable:

Apparel: *másli* (ribbon), *rékli* (jacket), *slicc* (fly), *stráf* (stripe), *stafírung* (wardrobe), *smink* (make-up), *smukk* (jewelry).

Kitchen and eating: *spájz* (pantry), *cuspájz* (dessert), *kredenc* (sideboard), *kuglóf* (cake), *smárni* (a type of dessert), *szaft* (juice), *nassol* (snacks), *vájdling* (mixing bowl).

Social activities: *kuglizik* (he bowls), *kókler* (impostor), *frakk* (tails), *parkett* (dance floor), *kujon* (rake), *vicc* (joke).

Military: In the Austro-Hungarian Army: *felcser* (medic), *front* (front), *sturm* (attack), *manóver* (maneuver), *faszol* (confiscate), *matróz* (sailor).

Hungary entered World War I on the side of the Monarchy. The 1920 Trianon Peace Treaty, following World War I, reduced the area of the country by approximately two-thirds of its former size, and approximately 3.3 million Hungarians found themselves in new countries ("The border crossed over us", as those affected said.) The Trianon Treaty was referred to in Hungary as a "Peace Ultimatum," and its results were compared with the disaster of Mohács. The change in borders and large groups of Hungarian-speaking populations finding themselves in different countries created serious linguistic and linguistic-political problems. (Bilingual problems, dispossessions, persecutions, limitations imposed on teaching and using their native language, restrictions in using Hungarian personal and place names, the ban on using Hungarian national symbols, etc.).

The "Discovery" of the Hungarian Language

During the Middle Ages and after, the legal and official language – the Lingua Patriae – of Hungary was Latin. It is impossible to speak about Hungarian as the national language even in theory until 1844 and in practice until 1867. The Hungarian language, although several thousand years old, did not serve as the official national language until the middle of the 19th century, except in a very limited way. At the time when the country was first established, there had to be a veritable linguistic Babel at the court of St. Stephen, just like in other medieval courts. A whole army of interpreters had to assist the work of the chancellery. In medieval Hungary, for all practical purposes, Latin was raised to the level of the national language. Latin was the language of politics, of legislation, of science and of the medieval universities. (Hence the referral to Latin as the *"deák",* or "classical" language.)

For a long period of time, Latin was the language of official communications and served as a lingua franca among the various polyglot groups. Latin was the language used in every-day communication among the higher classes. Hungarian was spoken only in the smaller Hungarian rural towns and villages and within the families.

The languages of the foreign settlers were used depending on local conditions. Since in medieval Hungary there was considerable regional administrative autonomy, there were a number of regions were the administration was exercised in different languages. In the Saxon cities of the Szepesség, the administrative language was German or Polish and in the Transylvanian Saxon cities, the administrative language was German. Linguistic assimilation was multidirectional. In many areas we may speak of a Hungarian take-over, but in the Felvidék, for instance, there are data suggesting that Slovakian had made appreciable inroads. The Hungarian language was used universally only in the Hungarian areas (primarily rural towns and villages). It was Latin that held the country together, it was the *lingua patriae* (national language). In the areas occupied and administrated by the Turks, a Hungarian-Turkish pidgin language evolved to provide for the required minimal communication needs. Thus, like in other European countries, a strange polyglot system developed in Hungary, too.

Language area	Latin	Hungarian or other
Diplomacy	+	
Schools	+	
Diplomas	+	
Chronicles and gestes	+	
Literature	+	
Legends	+	+ after 1372
Preaching	+	(+)
Folk poetry		+
Family, village		+
Compact nationality areas		+
Verbal directions to subordinates		+

In 1784 Joseph II replaced Latin with German as the official language of the Habsburg Empire. This practical edict raised a tremendous storm and it is from this time on that in Hungary and in other parts of the Empire the problem of a national language was linked with nationality issues, human rights and human dignity. In 1790, Joseph II withdrew the edict. Yet, after the turmoil caused by the language issue, a linguistic battle developed to replace the unifying, neutral, but dead Latin with living national languages. At the early 19th century National Assemblies, during the Reform Age, the language issue was the principal matter for discussion. In 1844, Hungarian became the official national language. After the defeat of the 1848 revolution and freedom fight, there was a return to a forceful and purposeful Germanization. It was only after the "Compromise" of 1867 that Hungarian again became the official national language. There would have been an opportunity between 1867 and 1918 for the other nationalities to share in all the national prerogatives achieved by the Hungarians. Unfortunately the national interests of the Hungarians and those of the other nationalities drifted further apart. The other nationalities started their own battles in order to have their own national languages officially recognized. This, among other things, led to the end of the Monarchy and to the dismemberment of Hungary following World War I. After the Trianon Peace Treaty, the successor states (Czechoslovakia, Romania and Yugoslavia) developed their own, hitherto unresolved national language policy issues which were characteristic of the last years of the Monarchy. The recent further division of some of the successor states have still not found a satisfactory solution to these vexing problems. As a consequence of this inability to cope with the problem, at the end of the 20th century there is an ongoing language war with and among the minorities in Slovakia, Romania and Lesser Yugoslavia.

Polyglottism in the Carpathian Basin:
Polyglottism is a millennial problem in the Carpathian Basin. The cities are bilingual. Hungarian soldiers are led by German commands in the Austrian army. In the early 1800s, German was more widely heard in the streets of Pest than Hungarian. Pozsony (after 1920 Bratislava) was a German-Hungarian-Slovakian city. Hungarian aristocrats rarely spoke Hungarian. Their daughters had German or French governesses and their sons learned western languages during extended study tours in the west. They used Hungarian only when addressing menials (nurses, hostlers, etc.). István Széchenyi, honored with the title of

"the greatest Hungarian" wrote his diary in German and as a young man spoke only broken Hungarian. To this day, the inability to roll the letter *r* is considered to be an aristocratic trait by the average Hungarian.

One memorial to this polyglottism, hardly flattering to either German or Hungarian reads: "The well-born man of the world speaks German to his dog, English to his horse, Hungarian to his coachman, French to his mistress, and Spanish to his God."

The emancipation of the Hungarian language and its elevation to the status of an official national language was the accomplishment of the minor nobility and of the gentry, who lived side by side with the ordinary people, of the Latinizing intellectuals, of the non-noble professional classes (teachers, engineers, lawyers, physicians), of the Hungarian officers serving at the Viennese Court and of the bourgeoisie whose sentiments were favorable toward Hungary and the Hungarians. It was this large group that revived the popular traditions, habits, dance, music, folksongs and folk-poetry. They were the ones who supported a national literature, theater, art and science and all of it based on the Hungarian language. Occasionally aristocrats also participated. György Bessenyei was a writer, who earlier in his life served as a Guard Officer for the Empress Maria Theresa, who absorbed the culture of the Viennese Court and who wrote essays strongly supporting the scientific development of the Hungarian language. "Every nation became learned in its own language, never in a foreign tongue. When the Hungarian peasant women talk Hungarian, their men will talk Hungarian as well. Similarly, when the serfs speak Hungarian, the gentlemen can not afford to forget the language." A renewal of the language was an integral component in the plans to establish a Hungarian national culture and may well have been the most important factor in the evolutionary movement.

The Academic "Discovery" of the Hungarian Language:

The first data leading to the scientific discovery of the Hungarian language were provided by Arabic, Byzantine and Western historians. We find Hungarian linguistic examples in a Latin grammatical text written by John Huss, the leader of the Czech Hussites, in 1412. Marcio Galeotto, the learned humanist at King Mátyás's court noticed the practically unique uniformity of the Hungarian language. When compared with the many and various dialects seen in Italy, he was struck by the fact that in Hungary the nobles and the lower orders all spoke the same way, used the same "dialect", the same words, the same expressions and even the same accent. The outstanding poet of that age, Janus Pannonius had studied in Italy, before being appointed bishop of Pécs. He wrote his poems in Latin, but there are some written indications that he also wrote a Hungarian grammar. Had it survived, it would have been the first such work in any European national language.

The domestic discovery of the Hungarian language also got its start during the era of humanism. It was one of Erasmus's basic educational principles that the great writers should be read only after the reader was familiar with the grammatical principles and rules of his native language. It was on the basis of these guidelines that interest in the structure of the "vulgar" languages developed, naturally on the Greek and Latin model. The first Hungarian "grammatical" work, i.e., a work containing some Hungarian grammatical comments was Hegendorf's *Rudimenta,* published in Cracow in 1527. The Hungarian references in this work were written by János Sylvester. He is considered to be the first Hungarian linguist, who according to the custom of the times was an expert in many areas. In 1534 he was invited by Tamás Nádasdy, a large landowner in Sárvár (formerly Újsziget) to act as a tutor in the family. Sylvester teaches, establishes a printing press, writes a

Latin-Hungarian grammar in Latin (actually more Hungarian than Latin), and translates and publishes the New Testament. He proves that the Hungarian language is suitable not only for the ancient, accented poetry but is perfectly capable of producing classic "metric" poetry as well. His couplets used the archaic "*i*" dialect but are fully understandable:

> *Az ki zsidóul és görögül és végre diákul*
> *Szól vala rígen, szól néked az itt magyarul.*
> *Minden népnek az ü nyelvin, hogy minden az isten*
> *Törvényin íljen, minden imádja nevit.*
> *Itt vagyon az rejtek kincs, itt vagyon az kifolyó víz.*
> *Itt vagyon a tudomány, mely örök íleted ád.*

(„He who spoke in Hebrew, Greek and finally in Latin a long time ago, speaks to you now in Hungarian. He speaks to each nation in its own language, so that they live by God's Commandments and so that all shall glorify His name. Here is the hidden treasure, here is the gushing spring, here is the science that gives eternal life.")

Sylvester notes and records the differences between Hungarian and the Indo-European languages. He likens Hungarian to Hebrew (after his sojourn in Sárvár, he was professor of Hebrew at the University of Vienna). He finds some similarities between the two languages, mainly in the area of the verbal personal suffixes, possessive nouns and the single-word causative verbs (so-called "*hiffil*" verbs). Sylvester was the first linguistic innovator who coined grammatical terms, e.g.: *névértvaló* - today *névmás* (pronoun), *beszédhezvaló* - today *határozószó* (adverb), *egybefoglaló* - today *kötőszó* (conjunction), etc. He also recommended the replacement of the Latin names for the months with Hungarian terms, e.g.: *böjtelő* (March), *böjtmás* (April), etc. In old Hungarian calendars we may encounter the Sylvestrian nomenclature, but the Hungarian language maintained that traditional Latin names for the months.

The borders of the mighty Ottoman Empire were only a stone's throw away from Sárvár and yet, the landowner establishes a school, a printing press and invites a humanist of European standing to his manor. In another part of the country, and again only a few kilometers from the Turks, at Gönc and Vizsoly, in County Abaúj, Gáspár Károlyi translates the Bible and has it printed in 1590. It is known as the *Vizsoly Bible.* This was the first complete translation of the Scriptures and it is still used in the Protestant ritual. Albert Szenczi Molnár who assisted at the birth of the Vizsoly Bible, published his Hungarian-Latin dictionary in 1604 and his Hungarian grammar in 1608, the latter for the primary purpose of making Hungarian accessible to foreigners. Later on, he translates the Psalms, a number of which are still sung during the Reformed Divine services. After several fragmentary manuscript 16th century grammars, we have the 1585 Calepinus 10 language dictionary, which was published in Lyons and which contains several tens of thousands of Hungarian words and expressions. In his book *Magyar Grammatikátska* (Small Hungarian Grammar), István Geleji Katona wishes to consolidate the wide spectrum of Hungarian spelling into a single system (Gyulafehérvár, 1645).

It was thus that the scientific and practical discovery of the Hungarian language got started in the 15th and 16th centuries. There are already Hungarian poets, writers, scientists, printing presses, schools (since 1635 a University), bibles, grammars, dictionaries and collections of sayings. The most talented young men study at the Universities of Western-Europe. Miklós Misztótfalusi Kis studies the printing trade at the famous Blaeu printers in Amsterdam. He became such an outstanding printer that he was deluged with orders from all of Europe. On request of the King of Georgia (Grusia), he prepared the first Grusian alphabet and with the money so earned, he printed a revised edition of the *Gáspár Károlyi Bible* in Amsterdam, in 1685.

During this period, the Reformation was spreading like wild-fire throughout the country and Transylvania became almost entirely Protestant. It is a beautiful example of Transylvanian tolerance that, according to an edict of 1568, there was the full freedom to practice the four religions (Catholic, Lutheran, Calvinist and Unitarian). This was the first such Act of Toleration in Europe and it produced a religious tolerance and peace that existed only in the far distant Holland.

The Birth of Literary Language:

Hungarian literary language had its start at the end of the 16th century and was a combination of the dialects of the north-eastern and other areas, reaching in a crescent-shaped region from Gömör via Abaúj, Zemplén, Ung, Bereg, Szatmár, Szabolcs, Bihar and Kraszna all the way to County Krassó-Szörény. The Tudós Társaság (Scientific Association), the predecessor of the Hungarian Academy of Sciences, was established in 1830 as the result of the Reform Period endeavors to advance the nation and its language. It immediately started the publication of the rules of orthography and of the dictionary of regional dialects.

During the period of Enlightenment interest increasingly focused on linguistic kinships. Albert Szenczi Molnár still considered the Hungarian language to be without any kinships, but it was soon thereafter that the first investigations into the Finno-Ugrian and later into the Turkish kinships were born.

The Language of the Reform Movement:

During the last quarter of the 18th century, namely during the period of Enlightenment, the development of the Hungarian language, literature, of general education and of the sciences became a national program. Writers contributed by translating foreign works and scientists by writing about their studies in Hungarian. It turned out that the Hungarian language was not really suitable for this purpose. Under the leadership of Ferenc Kazinczy (writer and poet, 1759-1831), a movement began to renew and enrich the Hungarian language and to work out a linguistic ideal and a working norm. National awakening was accompanied by similar attempts to develop and beautify the national language in France, in Germany, in Greece and later in Turkey.

The Hungarian linguistic renewal, starting in the 1770s lasted almost for a century, peaking during the early 1800s. The center of the movement was Ferenc Kazinczy's home in Széphalom, near Sátoraljaújhely, in County Zemplén. The fight between the neologists (favoring language reform), and the orthologists (opposing language reform) captured the attention of the public for an extensive period of time. In 1813 the orthologists published an anonymous pamphlet entitled *Mondolat* (Statement) in which they made fun of the language reform group. In response to this challenge, Kazinczy's friends, Ferenc Kölcsey (the author of the National Anthem), and Pál Szemere published the *Felelet* (The Answer) in 1815. The debate was not free of personal comments; one language reformer, Dávid Barczafalvi Szabó, the editor of the *Magyar Hírmondó* (Hungarian News Chronicler) was labeled "a notorious language destroyer," to which accusation he modestly responded be saying: "I am not as bad as my reputation." In fact, of his 400 word changes, 80 are alive and well even today.

The favorite passtime of another language reformer was shortening words. E.g.: *cukorsüteményes = cukrász*

141

(confectioner), *seborvos* = *sebész* (surgeon), *gépely* = *gép* (machine). This reformer represented a general linguistic trend, namely an inherent philological economy, i.e., a tendency toward thrift and brevity. This actually fits in well with the "quick-talk" characteristic of the current, digitalized mass-communication "revolution" which a witty Dutch linguist has termed "turbo-talk". One of its cardinal word manipulations is indeed shortening the existing words.

Another favorite word-modifying practice of the language reformers was the combination of words, which was also a word-shortening process:

cső + *orr* → **csőr** (tube + nose → beak)
könnyű + *elméjű* → **könnyelmű** (light + minded → light-headed, rash)
levegő + *ég* → **lég** (air + heaven → air, atmosphere)
rovátkolt + *barom* → **rovar** (grooved + animal → insect)
híg + *anyag* → **higany** (thin + material → mercury)

In addition to the above mentioned word contractions, the most productive expansion of the vocabulary consisted of the creation of new words, corresponding to new concepts. This was done either from scratch or by combining existing words. Prior to this time, the Hungarian language preferred to enrich itself by the creation of new words. In the early Hungarian texts we can find practically no composite words.

The appearance of composite words coincides with the renewal period of the language and is today a frequent method of creating new words. E.g.:

folyóirat (running+writing → periodical, review)
helyesírás (correct+writing → orthography)
jellemrajz (character + sketch → character study, profile)
rendőr (order+guard → policeman)

Favorite language renewal modifiers were *-szt: fagy-aszt* (freeze), *fogy-aszt* (consumes), *törl-eszt* (amortize); *-sít: mozgó-sít* (mobilize), *fiú-sít* (masculinize); *-alom/-elem: bánt-alom* (ailment, affront), *győz-elem* (victory); *-mány/-mény: állít-mány* (predicate), *él-mény* (experience). The more important formatives created by the language renewers were: *-c, bohó-c* (clown), *él-c* (jest); *-nc: fegy-enc* (convict), *lel-enc* (foundling), *ifj-onc* (youngster), *kegy-enc* (favorite).

They "severed" the *-da* syllable from existing words like *csárda* (tavern), *kaloda* (pillory), and took the *-da/-de* formative that could be applied to almost any word and which, in fact, produced a large number of new words, primarily designating a location or place of business. E.g.: *áruda* (store), *bölcsőde* (nursery), *cukrászda* (pastry shop), *csónakda* (boathouse), *dalárda* (glee club), *fagylalda* (ice cream parlor), *iroda* (office), *járda* (sidewalk), *képezde* (school), *kóroda* (hospital, today *kórház*), *lovarda* (riding academy), *lövölde* (shooting gallery), *nyomda* (printery), *óvoda* (kindergarten), *öntöde* (foundry), *pénzverde* (mint), *sütöde* (bakery), *szálloda* (hotel), *szövöde* (knitting mill), *tanoda* (school), *távirda* (telegraph office), *tébolyda* (asylum), *tőzsde* (stock exchange), *uszoda* (swimming pool), *vizelde* (urinal), and *zárda* (convent). Many of these words can be found today on fascia boards in the streets.

The innovators also took **regional dialect terms** and introduced them into the regular language. E.g.: *betyár* (highwayman), *burgonya* (potato), *hús* (meat), *kandalló* (fireplace), and *róna* (flat plain). Other regional words popularized were *csűr* (barn), *szénatartó* (hay loft), and *rekeszték* (hiding place), which more recently was replaced by *páholy,* meaning a box in a theater.

Old **Hungarian names** were also brought back into use, e.g.: *Ákos, Árpád, Béla, Géza, Gyula* and *Zoltán.* It

143

may be noted in every language that the name of the protagonists in the works of famous writers becomes quite popular.

Hungarian writers and poets also invented names that became very popular. E.g.: András Dugonics, the first Hungarian novelist, coined *Jolán* (from *jóleányka* = good girl), Mihály Vörösmarty coined *Hajna, Csilla, Tünde* and *Dalma* (the last was originally a man's name but became a female name later on). János Arany coined *Gyöngyvér* in the Csaba trilogy, but also popularized the old names of *Attila, Csaba* and *Ildikó.*

In some instances the innovators disturbed the traditional structure of the Hungarian language. Hungarian grammatical instinct rebels if a suffix ending a word, has an additional formative tacked on to it. Yet the innovators did just that and, at times, successfully. E.g.: *kézbe-sít* → *kézbesít* (into the hand give → deliver), *szembe-sít* (confront). It is odd, but one of the words created at that time, still sounds strange to a Hungarian ear. The word is *ki-akolbólít*, meaning to expel from the corral, to oust. It is worth while to examine this strange word: *ki+akol+ból+ít* – verbal prefix + noun + adverbial suffix + verbal formative. Even though only the *akolból* (from the corral) sounds right, the whole word is still used, albeit rarely.

The results of the linguistic innovations were scientifically gathered together at the end of the 19th century. Of the words introduced or created by the innovators, about 10,000 are currently in regular use. The words introduced or created by the innovators were immediately accepted and used by the greatest Hungarian writers and poets of the period (Mihály Vörösmarty, János Arany, Sándor Petőfi, Mór Jókai), and thus they were also acepted by the general public. The innovators were guided not only by considerations of utility but also by esthetic principles.

They were seeking for euphonia, i.e., they wanted the language to be attractive. The enormous accomplishments of the linguistic innovators were achieved without any official governmental assistance and were motivated purely by enthusiasm and by an almost unlimited endeavor to improve and advance the Hungarian language. This moral stance and its remarkable achievements served as an inducement to later generations of linguistic movers and shakers. The greatest achievement of the innovators, however, was that they managed to make the Hungarian language into a developed, modern instrument and that it gave the man in the street the experience and the excitement of linguistic innovation and evolution.

Hungarian Linguistic "Travel"

Dialects:

The Hungarian language is relatively free of dialectal variations. None of them cause significant problems in comprehension, like they do in Germany or in the United Kingdom.

Many believe that this is due to the fact that Hungary has a relatively limited area. Yet the area inhabited by Hungarian speaking people is not that small. Prior to 1920, Hungary had an area of 283 thousand square kilometers and its current area is 93 thousand square kilometers. Hungarian was and is spoken in this entire area. The distance from Holland to Sopron is almost the same as from Sopron to Sepsiszentgyörgy in present-day Romania, at the other end of the Hungarian language area. We are talking of a distance of approximately 700 - 1000 kilometers. The longest train ride in the Austro-Hungarian Monarchy, from Volóc in the Kárpátalja to Fiume in the present Croatia, was just about 1,000 kilometers (625 miles). In other countries major dialectal differences are found in substantially smaller areas.

The Hungarian dialects have been studied thoroughly by linguists and there are a number of dialectal dictionaries (e.g.: the Ormánság Dictionary, the Szeged Dictionary, the Slavonia-Kórógy Dictionary, the Palóc Dictionary and the New Hungarian Dialectal Dictionary). There is also a linguistic map that shows the characteristics of the Hungarian dialects displayed on the pages of a dialectal atlas.

In some of the Hungarian dialects, certain sounds are used which are not common in the regular language and which add a certain variability to the regional speech. In some dialects diphthongs are used, e.g.: for *kéz* (hand) - *kiéz* or *kéiz* and for *volt* (was) - *voult* or *vuolt*. The Palóc, living at the northern edge of the language area, pronounce the *a* sound with the archaic almost closed lips, instead of the generally used *a* sound pronounced with open and rounded lips. Wherever the Palóc move to, they take this characteristic sound with them. In the area beyond the Tisza and in parts of Transdanubia the *é* sound is replaced by an *i* sound: *kík* for *kék* (blue), *szíp* for *szép* (lovely), and *nígy* for *négy* (four). In some of the dialects a distinction is made between the open *e* sound and the closed *e* sound (western Transdanubian, Tisza, Palóc and Székely). In some parts of the south, most typically in Hódmezővásárhely and Szeged, the closed *e* sound is replaced by an *ö* sound, e.g.: *embör* for *ember* (man), *föstő* for *festő* (painter), *mögreped* for *megreped* (split), *ölég* for *elég* (enough), *lösz* for *lesz* (will be), and *föst* for *fest* (he paints). The *Szeged* (i.e. *Szöged*) dialectal peculiarity has almost risen to the level of a literary language and the first Hungarian novelist, András Dugonics, in his novel *Etelka,* originally used this dialect. When he noticed the disapproval of the linguistic innovators, he rewrote the novel, using the standard pronunciation. Zsigmond Móricz, in his novel about Sándor Rózsa, the Szeged-area highwayman, has his hero speak in the typical *"ö"* dialect. The same is true for the novel *Por* (Dust) by Ferenc Temesi, several of whose chapters are located in the Szeged area.

There are also dialectal differences in the length of certain sounds. In the western and Transdanubian dialect, the use of the long vowels is much more restricted, e.g.: *husz* for *húsz* (twenty), *tiz* for *tíz* (ten), and *biru* for *bíró* (judge). The opposite is true in the Tisza dialect where we are likely to find longer vowels than in the standard speech, e.g.: *tanúlt* for *tanult* (he learned).

Some of the students of the dialects have noted a difference in the rate of speech. Accordingly, the eastern Hungarians speak more slowly and deliberately, while the western Hungarians speak more rapidly and briskly. In the northern Palóc dialect the archaic *ly (lj)* sound is still very much alive.

Some of the morphologic differences in the dialects are based on acoustic differences. A Palóc will say good-by with *letesletjobbakat* (all the very best) instead of the standard *legeslegjobbakat*. The sign for the superlative in the standard language is *legesleg-*, while in the Palóc dialect it is *leteslet-*. There are also peculiar regional dialectal expressions. In the north, they say: *Gyere nálunk* instead of *Gyere el hozzánk* (Come to us); *Elment a bírónál* instead of *Elment a bíróhoz* (He went to the judge). The standard *hoz/-hez/-höz* is replaced by *-nál/-nél*. Yet another example: *Erzsi, dobd le útlevelet!* for *Erzsi, dobd le az útlevelet!* (Erzsi throw down passport (omitting the article).

In some dialects, words are used that are not used anywhere else. This becomes immediately obvious. For instance, the name for the small local commuter trains is *göcse* in Komárom, *zsuzsi* in Debrecen, *csángó-vasút* in Vágselye and Mátyusföld, while in yet other places they may use *kávédaráló* (coffee grinder), *madzagvasút* (rubber band train), *fatengelyes* (wood axle), etc. *Kacsa* (duck) may become *kácsa* in the west, *réce* in the east, and *ruca* in Transylvania. *Töpörtyű* (cracklings) may become *tepertő* or *töpörtő* in the east, and *pörc* or *pörke* along the Balaton. The *fánk* (doughnut) becomes *pánkó* in the east and in Transylvania, and *pampuska* or *siska* in the north. What is known in Budapest as *töltött káposzta* (stuffed cabbage) is called *szárma* in the south.

The major Hungarian dialects are as follows:

1. ***Western.*** Győr-Moson-Sopron. It includes parts of Counties Vas, Zala and Veszprém. Within this area, we may mention the dialects of Rábaköz (Kapuvár,

148

Csorna and Mihályi), Felsőőr (Oberwart in Austria), Őrség (Őriszentpéter), Göcsej (west of Zalaegerszeg). In this area the vowels *i* and *u* are short: *víz* (water), and *kut* (well).

2. *Transdanubia.* Counties Veszprém, Somogy, Fejér and Tolna as well as Csallóköz and Mátyusföld in Slovakia. In this area, the *a* is frequently pronounced like an *ó: házba - házbó* (into the house).

3. *Southern and Great Plains.* The entire southern part of Hungary. This area is characterized by the use of the sound *ö*. The area includes Kalocsa and Szeged, famous for their paprika and Makó, celebrated for its onions.

4. *Tisza.* The Tisza was known once as the most Hungarian of all rivers, since its springs are in Hungary and it empties into the Danube. The area includes the regulated waterways of the Tisza, the Körös and the Berettyó rivers as well as the southern parts of Counties Szolnok, Bihar and Hajdú.

5. *Palóc.* This area includes the northern areas of Hungary and the southern part of Slovakia, between the rivers Vág and Hernád. The characteristic dialects are: the Matyó (Mezőkövesd), the Palóc of Nógrád (the enchanting world of writer Kálmán Mikszáth), the Barkó (Putnok area). Easily identified by the illabial *a* sound.

6. *North-east.* Includes counties Abaúj, Zemplén, Szabolcs, Szatmár and Bereg. This area is the birth-place of the Hungarian literary language.

7. *Mezőség.* The central part of the Hungarian area of Romania. It includes Kalotaszeg, Kolozsvár, Torda and Maros, all celebrated for their native arts.

8. *Székely.* In Romania, mostly in counties Háromszék, Udvarhely and Brassó. The archaic past tenses and the *-ik* conjugation are still practiced in this area.

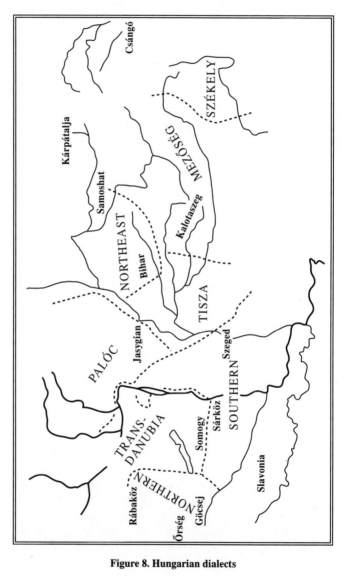

Figure 8. Hungarian dialects

There are Hungarian language areas which for historic reasons became separated from the Hungarian core language area. These are known as linguistic islands. Two such linguistic islands are:

1. *Csángó.* A Hungarian group residing beyond the crest of the Carpathians in Moldavia. Their name is derived from a Székely dialect term: *csáng,* meaning separated or wandered off. Their center is in Bákó (Bacau). The linguistic renewal and enrichment did not penetrate to the Csángó linguistic island. Their language is practically identical with the Hungarian spoken in ancient times.

2. *Slavonian linguistic island.* Four villages in the neighborhood of Eszék. During the Yugoslav conflict of 1991-1995, these villages were largely destroyed.

Linguistic and folkloristic curiosities emerge from the Hungarian dialects and folk tales even to this day. It was found that a collection of lullabies took a central position between the European northern and southern lullaby traditions. Ancient incantations can be still collected today and so can magic texts to ward off illness. In the 1970s Zsuzsanna Erdélyi's collection created a sensation when it was realized that it contained archaic (perhaps pre-Christian) folk prayers, several of them in "ancient Hungarian".

The Language of Budapest:

In the 19th century, the capital began to play an increasingly important role. At the beginning of the century it still consisted of three small adjacent cities, Pest, Buda and Óbuda. The first permanent bridge across the Danube was opened in 1848 and still stands today. It was built on the urging of István Széchenyi and is known as the Chain Bridge. At the time of the 1848 freedom fights, only about one-third of the population was Hungarian. In the streets German predominated. *Milimárik (millimárik,* milkmaids) were selling milk: *Káfen's a Milli und an Obers-Kaufen Sie eine Milch und ein Obers* – Buy milk and cream. One could often hear the cry *Dónavósz (Donauwasser –* Danube water), and *Káfnz sooond (Kaufen Sie Sand –* Buy sand). The people were reading a *ceitung (Zeitung –* newspaper) in the *káféhausz (Kaffeehaus –* café), and drank *brudersaft (Bruderschaft –* brotherhood, friendship) to each other.

The individual cities of Buda, Pest and Óbuda were united into Budapest in 1873. At that time the city consisted of 10 districts. In 1950, Greater Budapest was established with 22 (currently 23) districts. The increase in the population of the capital was dramatic:

1869	302,059
1910	1,110,439
1949	1,590,316
1992	2,015,955.

Today, 20% of the country's population lives in Budapest, and if we include the metropolitan area, the percentage rises to 30%.

During the second half of the 19th century, Budapest played an increasingly important role in the unification and standardization of the language. The process of combining the various dialects and reforming the language started in the north-east, but the process was transferred to Budapest, where the language was further simplified and assumed a slightly different tonality as "Budapest Hungarian". The diphthongs used in the dialects were never accepted in the written language and now were eliminated from the language spoken in Budapest as well. In the 19th century there were still two *j* and two *e* sounds. In spelling we have preserved the dual form of *ly* and *j,* but in the Budapest Hungarian and, indeed, in the spoken language everywhere, both forms are pronounced as *j*.

The mass media (uniformly located in Budapest) use the *j* and open *e* sound and dialects are heard only extremely rarely in any public communication. Among politicians, dialects may be heard occasionally, in the mass media, never. In the Budapest cabarets and, later on the radio and in television, the use of a dialect denoted ignorance and backwardness. If a cabaret writer wished to present a person as a primitive character, he was made to talk in a dialect (frequently a phony one). Budapest thus assumed a strong homogenizing linguistic role.

Yet, even within the city, there was an internal territorial "dialectal division". In the early 1900s, the linguist, Géza Bárczi described the appearance of "urban dialects". He found that they were speaking differently in the Ferencváros than in the Angyalföld (two fairly distant urban districts). In the Ferencváros there were many German loan-words, while in Újpest and in the Városliget different suffixes gained popularity. We can find some traditional dialectal characteristics in the language of Budapest, particularly in the older districts which were incorporated into the city only in 1950. There are still some small town and even village features in some of these areas, such as Nagytétény, Békásmegyer, Újpest, Cinkota, Soroksár, Rákospalota, Rákosszentmihály and Rákoskeresztúr. In the north-east corner of Budapest there is a small area which abuts on a region where a strange Palóc dialect can still be heard.

The most characteristic feature of the language of Budapest, however, is the language of the underworld (thieves' argot and "jazz-talk"), which is inseparable from metropolitan life. There is also a slang which appears in all large cities and which radiates a lightheartedness, an irony and a great deal of humor. The bases for the Budapest argot and slang are the German, Hebrew and Gypsy languages. The kind of German spoken commonly in

153

Budapest at the beginning of the 19th century has been largely relegated to the kitchen (*speiz* - pantry, *sámli* - footstool, *sufni* - lean-to and *hokedli* - ottoman), and has been debased to an argot.

Some characteristic words and where they come from are listed below.

Words of German origin:
Grund – lot, plot (used in Ferenc Molnár's famous
      novel, *The Boys of Paul Street*)
peisli – lung
smóci (today *smaci*) – kiss
hári - hair
baci (today *bazi*) – large
tróger – laborer
fater – father
muter – mother
spíler – card cheat

From German thieves' argot:
fuksz – gold
link – unreal, phony, unreliable
firol – cheat, mislead
iberöl – hand over

Hebrew and Yiddish elements:
meló – work
mázli – good luck
kajah (today *kajak*) – strength
mesüge – nuts
haver – pal, buddy
jatt – hand, also a tip
hirig – fisticuffs

Gypsy (Romany) words:
máró – bread
duma – talk
dilinós – crazy
piál – he drinks
basavál – he makes music
lóvé – money
lugnya-luvnya – bad woman
csávó – boy
csaj, *spiné* – girl
lácsó – good
kamel – he loves
halóz – he eats
mafta (today *nafta*) – gasoline
szajre (today *szajré*) – stolen goods

Other languages:
frankó – good (from the Italian)
durmol – he sleeps (from the Italian)
bulanzser – baker (from the French)

Distorted words:
zri – confusion, noise, entertainment (from the *Zrínyi*
        Street police station)
satyak – cap (from *sapka*)
lizsé – park (from *liget*)

Abbreviations:
lé – money (from *leves* - soup)
mó – movies (from *mozi*)
dö – forest (from *erdő*)
uccso – last (from *utolsó*)
zsé – policeman (from *zsaru*)
szaki – Socialist (from *szocialista*)
komcsi – Communist (from *kommunista*)

Some characteristic expressions:

Felkaptam a vizet – I got mad (literally: I took on the water)

Gáz lesz – There will be trouble (literally: there will be gas)

Megcsípem magamnak – I will get to know her/him (literally: I will pinch/grab her/him for myself).

One of the best characteristics of the language of Budapest is the humor of its inhabitants. Next to Berlin, Prague and Vienna, Budapest is considered the joke center of Central-Europe. The jokes of Budapest are current, political, critical, sharp, stinging, occasionally crude, and contain numerous linguistic virtuosities (word-plays and tricks). Here is a small sample:

The first transportation joke (horse drawn trams were established in 1866 and electric trams in 1887):
"Conductor, could you not go any faster?"
"I sure could, but I can't leave this damn contraption!"

In 1927 a young man is explaining the principle of the radio to his aunt in Debrecen:
"Imagine that you have a dog as large as the distance from Budapest to Debrecen. When I step on his tail here, you hear him bark in Debrecen. Well, that's radio, just without the dog."

A lawyer's office in the fall of 1944:
"How much for a divorce from my wife?"
"Forty pengős."
"Forty pengős? Are you crazy?! For 50 pengős I can have her shot."

A café in Budapest in 1946:
"Boss, the coffee is so bad that the customers are threatening to beat us up."
"Don't worry, we outnumber them two to one."

In 1950 three men sit in a tavern. One spits on the floor, the second is all upset and says, "Pfui, you pig!" The third one says, "Please let's leave politics out of this."

Two men are having a chat:
"Do you whisper sweet nothings to your wife when you make love?"
"Well, if she happens to be there, why not?"

Traffic report:
"The M1, the M5 and the M7 routes are passable. The route to Lenin's socialism is not."

Cursing and Invectives in the Hungarian Language

From an earlier quotation we know that the well-born gentleman spoke Hungarian only to his coachman. However, this is little wonder. "The Hungarians are the world champion cursers". Such comments are rife in Hungary and other areas. According to a well-known expert in "cursology", "Yiddish has created the most inventive curses, but Hungarian the most complicated and coarsest ones."

The Hungarians seem to be proud of this fact, and Hungarian curses are numerous and various. The old curses are complex, long and involved, and are considered linguistic curiosities today. There are also short and primitive curses which are condemned by all more sensitive people. The introduction of obscenities into literature raised a major storm in the 1960s. In radio and television, sensitivity bans the use of obscenity. However, in Hungarian rap music there are both slang and obscene words.

Cursing is aggression expressed through language. It is an expression of agitation and anger, and contains blasphemy, obscenity and expressions designed to offend individuals and religious sentiments. One set of curses is always readily available and consists of linguistic clichés, which are frequently used as conversational fillers, without any particular emotions. Another set of curses consists of improvisations. Their function is similar to expletives – angry, partly involuntary mouthing. Their major groups are: blasphemy, invectives and oaths, and derogatory comments.

For how long have the Hungarians been cursing? There is one view according to which the Hungarians had brought cursing along on their migration from Asia.

According to others, cursing originated with the Serbs, while a majority holds the Turks responsible.

Some explain the use of curses as the manifestation of a peculiarly Hungarian psychological characteristic. The curser damns the higher authority from whom he has waited in vain for an answer to his prayers. A bitter self-destructive, Hungaro-pessimism is in fact a noticeable psychologic manifestation, a sort of national "sport".

An early name for cursing was "Heyduck talk". The "Hajdúk" were free cattle breeders and herdsmen and also served as mercenary troops. They lived beyond the central portion of the Tisza and apparently had a tough life and plenty of opportunities for cursing. It seems likely that the wars and the lengthy periods of military service were favorable for making cursing fashionable.

Beginning with the 15th century, we have written records of invectives and curses in letters, in literary remains and in the transcripts of witch trials. Among the early invectives we find *ördög teremtette* (it's the devil's work).Today we use *kutya teremtette* (it's the dog's work, the dog made it) as a very mild expletive. Whoever attributed creation to a dog or to a devil, rather than to God, was blaspheming God. There are records which show that until the 18th century, such blasphemy was punished with fines, dismissal from school, even 100 strokes with a cane, cutting out the tongue, even death.

Many curses took their origin from diseases. Certain expressions which seem fairly innocuous today, e.g.: *frász törjön ki, fene egye meg, rosseb vigye el,* and *nyavalya törje ki*, variations of "May you get the 'French' disease"), were clearly serious invectives which have largely lost their true meaning and are used quite widely today even in fairly polite society.

Hungarian curses may be divided according to the following scheme:

1. Mocking or denigrating intellectual or bodily ability: *hülye vagy* (you're an idiot), *béna vagy* (you're a cripple [mentally]).

2. Comparison with animals: *ökör vagy* (you're an ox), *patkány vagy* (you're a rat), *hazug disznó* (you're a lying pig).

3. Curses associated with body parts, particularly genitalia: *hülye picsa* (stupid cunt), *vén fasz* (old prick), *le van szarva* (shit on you).

4. Wishing an illness on somebody: *a pusztulás jöjjön rátok* (may you perish), *a rák egye ki a belit* (may cancer eat your gut).

5. Invectives against near relatives, particularly the mother: This was known as "mothering" and was considered serious enough to usually lead to physical violence: *kurva anyádat* (your mother the whore).

6. Blasphemy:

In a primitive environment, the most frequent conversational filler is what we euphemistically call "the F word". The dictionaries give no etymology for it, but the Hungarian variant appears for the first time in a document from 1221 and is probably a Turkic loan-word antedating the Conquest.

The convoluted, complex curses rich in verbal imagery, introduced by the writers, are unlikely to be encountered in the streets. In a critical situation we may hear a brief expletive or, more frequently, a slightly expurgated oath. In a primitive environment the *"baszd meg"* (fuck it) is heard as a conversation filler and is not meant to be offensive. The causes for the truly coarse, cursing expletives are an uncontrollable infuriating situation, a joy in breaking a taboo, or simply excessive linguistic permissiveness.

Curses are the phraseologic offshoots of the richness of the Hungarian language. Accompanying the traditional imagery, there is even today a rich new crop of proverbs and descriptive expressions. The Hungarian language is very rich in imagery, and this is reflected in the continuously produced new expressions and sayings. In many of these expressions, there are comparisons connected with the word *"like"*. E.g.: *Betakarlak, mint Moszkvát a hó* (I cover you like the snow covers Moscow), *Elterült, mint az ólajtó* (He fell flat like the door of a pigsty), *Elütlek, mint a hegyipásztort a lavina* (I will run you over like an avalanche runs over a mountain shepherd).

From the talk of soldiers and students we gather some jocular belittling expressions, usually beginning with: *Kevés vagy, mint…* (you're as little/insufficient/deficient [etc.] as… – you amount to no more than…). E.g.: *Kevés vagy mint a sivatagban a gémeskút* (There's as little of you as wells in a desert), *Kevés vagy, mint árvaházban a szülői értekezlet* (You're as much good as a PTA meeting in an orphanage).

There are humorous threats, usually beginning with *nehogy* (lest, don't let, it's like, make sure, etc.). These are frequently absurd, but very popular and spreading rapidly. E.g.: *Nehogy a nyúl vigye a puskát* (Don't let the rabbit carry the rifle), *Nehogy már a Lánchíd folyjon a Duna alatt* (Don't [tell me] it's Chain Bridge flowing under the Danube), *Nehogy már a befőtt rakja el a nagymamát* (Make sure it's not the pickle that preserves your grandmother).

Tradition and innovation are both alive and well in modern Hungarian phraseology. *Hátulról kezdik az esküvőt* ("They start the wedding from the back" – they live together without the benefit of the clergy), *Felkapja a vizet mint a szigmapumpa* ("He sucks up water like a pump" – he becomes angry), and *Ne szólj bele, nem telefon* ("Don't talk into it [interrupt], it's not a telephone") are just some of many amusing examples. When newly rich, dressed to kill, young men get out of a Mercedes in front of a disco, several people may comment sarcastically: "The village bulls have arrived." The village bull or communal bull was a jointly owned animal, used strictly for insemination.

Slang creates, renews and starts linguistic fashions. There is also a counterpart to slang, namely the dull, unimaginative banalities and clichés. These everyday usages and platitudes have been collected by Miklós Hernádi (*Közhelyszótár* – Dictionary of Clichés). It is also true, however that many of the clichés of the 1970s have recently reappeared, and are now thought of as witty.

The Hungarian Language and Politics

The Hungarian language very rapidly reflects the political, economic and social changes. Following 1948, "the year of the change," namely after the Communist take-over, a large number of words were eliminated from the Hungarian language. E.g.: *tőzsde* (stock exchange), *cseléd* (servant), *csendőr* (gendarmes), *cserkész* (Boy Scout), *dologház* (workhouse), *hadapródiskola* (cadet academy), *karpaszományos* (volunteer military officer), *kegydíj* (civil-list pension), *lelencház* (foundling home), *levente* (paramilitary youth organization), *ludovikás* (Military Academy Student), *menhely* (alms-house), *nagybirtok* (estate), *népkonyha* (soup kitchen), *nyilvánosház* (brothel), *szegényház* (poor-house), *tolncház* (detention barracks), *úriember* (gentleman), and *városatya* (city father).

The previous system's forms of address also disappeared: *méltóságos* (worshipful), *kegyelmes* (excellency), *tekintetes* (honorable), *nagyságos úr/asszony* (your grace).

Similarly to other countries, in Hungary, too, the communist system (1948-1989) created its own vocabulary. During the 1950s there was a veritable "semantic revolution". The words departed from their original meaning and took on several new meanings. Orwellian "newspeak" became a political reality in governmental publications. Ideology penetrated into everyday activities and even into interpersonal relationships. One of the catchwords of socialism was *béke* (peace). E.g.: *békekölcsön* (peace loan) – a mandatory monthly contribution between 1950 and 1956, actually a form of taxation. *Békefelhívás* (call for peace), *békeértekezlet* (peace conference), *békebizottság* (peace commission), *béke aláírás* (peace signature), *békeharc* (peace fight), *békepap* (peace priest – a cleric active in the Peace Movement), *béketábor* (Peace Camp), and *béketüntetés* (peace demonstration).

Common expressions of the era included: *polgári csökevény* (bourgeois remnant), *deklasszált elemek* (declassé elements [people]), both negative expressions for those belonging to the old upper classes. *Disszidál* (leaves unlawfully for abroad), *fellazító* (inflammatory – one who tends to weaken the "solid" Marxist-Leninist ideology), *harmadikutas* (third way traveler – one who favors an intermediary position between socialism and capitalism), *kollektivizálás* (collectivization), *tervgazdálkodás* (planned economy), and *össznépi* (something affecting the entire population).

The controlling position of a single party and its presence in all aspects of the political, economic and social life of the country are shown by the following compound words: *pártbizottság* (party committee), *pártaktíva* (party activist), *pártdemokrácia* (party democracy), *pártegység* (party unity), *pártépítés* (building the party), *párterdek* (party interest), *pártfeladat* (party responsibility), *pártfunkcionárius* (party functionary), *pártgyűlés* (party congress), *pártház* (party building), *pártkáder* (party cadre), *pártkritika* (party self-assessment), *pártonkívüli* (one outside of the party), *pártszervezet* (party organization), *pártvonal* (party line), etc., etc., etc.

Additional words from everyday life, but reflecting the period, include: *kulákföld* (kulak-owned land), *kultúrház* (house of culture), *osztályellenes* (class enemy), *államvédelem* (state security), *élmunkás* (shock-worker), *gyermekváros* (children's city), *határsáv* (frontier zone), *házkezelőség* (house management), *kisdobos* (pre-Pioneer child), *úttörő* (pioneer), *mintaszövetkezet* (model co-operative), *munka-érdemrend* (Order of Labor), *néphadsereg* (people's army), *szakérettségi* (graduation from trade school), *társbérlet* (co-tenancy), *termelőszövetkezet* (agricultural [producing] co-operative), *traktorállomás* (tractor stand), *házgyár* (house factory, i.e., factories making prefab panelling for apartment houses), *szputnyik* (sputnik), *bérrendezés* (rent control), *brigádmozgalom* (brigade movement), *függetlenített szakszervezeti titkár* (independent trade union secretary), *munkaverseny* (production competition), *sztahanovista* (stakhanovite), *termelési értekezlet* (production conference), *versenymozgalom* (competitive endeavor movement), and *zárszámadás* (final accounting).

Hungarian socialism was patterned after the Soviet model. Yet, its vocabulary did not include very many structural Russianizations. Even though Russian was the first (and often only) mandatory foreign language taught in Hungarian schools between 1949 and 1989, it contributed very little to the spread of Russian expressions in the language or, for that matter, to the learning of any foreign language. The language of officialdom, on the other hand, was suffused with a large number of expressions which were direct translations from the Russian. Thus, for instance, *községháza* (city hall) became the *tanácsház* (council house), and *miniszterelnök* (Prime Minister) became a *minisztertanács elnöke* (President of the Council of Ministers). There were numerous other terms derived from the Russian which began with "Soviet" or "council". The term: *egy sor* (a row of – meaning many) is taken from the Russian, and so is the verb *viszonyul* (relate to), which is used in expressions such as *"nem megfelelően viszonyul a munkájához"* (He does not relate properly to his work). Other terms translated from the Russian include *szűk keresztmetszet* (narrow cross section), and the conventional terms *drága barátaim* (my cherished friends), and *forró üdvözletem* (my ardent greetings).

Direct **Russian words** taken over into the popular language were generally words that had a negative connotation and expressed the average person's feelings about the Russians: *davaj* (let's go), *zabrál* (he loots), *apparatcsik* (a member of the system), *malenkij robot* (a little work – i.e., forced labor), *durák* (fool), *bumáska* (wallet), *nacsalnyik* (chief).

The political-economic changes in effect since 1989 have led to readjustments in the language as well. The political language has undergone spectacular changes. The earlier, simplified party jargon which frequently revealed a great lack of education, was replaced by a range of voices appropriate to a multi-party system. The old Hungarian political rhetorical traditions (flowery, circular sentences) were re-introduced. The young democrats introduced "turbo-speech" into politics, and demagogues also made their appearance. The paternalistic "we", so commonly used in the previously popular party jargon, disappeared for a while and the forms of address also underwent an appreciable change.

Popular expressions characteristic for the time of political change (slogans) included: *vállalati tanács* (industrial/company council), *kétszintű bankrendszer* (two-tiered banking system), *átképzési* (later *munkanélküli*) *segély* (retraining - later unemployment-assistance), *szociális védőháló* (social safety net), *jogállam* (constitutional state), *kibontakozási program* (developmental program), *pluralizmus* (pluralism), and *világútlevél* (world passport).

The economic changes also brought about changes in the vocabulary: *minimálbér* (minimum wage), *tőzsde* (stock exchange), *államkötvény* (government bonds), *adóalapcsökkentő értékpapír* (tax base reducing tax-free shares), *privatizáció* (privatization, creation of private property), *kárpótlás* (compensation), *valutatartalék* (foreign exchange reserves), *forintleértékelés* (forint devaluation), and *brókercég menedzser* (brokerage house manager).

The remodeled governmental system also required a number of new terms: *államminiszter* (state minister), *tárca nélküli miniszter* (minister without portfolio), *önkormányzat* (self-, or local government), *polgármesteri hivatal* (mayoral office), *városháza* (city hall), *községháza* (village hall), and *köztársasági megbízott* (a representative of the republic).

Greetings and Forms of Address

The system of greetings and addresses has always created a complex linguistic muddle in the Hungarian language. They changed from time to time and their stylistic significance also underwent changes. An address that may have been improper or incorrect in the past is now correct and proper, and the reverse is also possible. These complex rules are frequently violated even by native Hungarians.

The Hungarian language distinguishes between an address in the second and third person singular and plural. An address in the second person is simple, and there is only one way of saying it. In the third person, however, there are three options of various shades of meaning and courtesy. Initially, there was probably only a second person address (in prayers God is addressed in the second person and in obituaries the departed is usually referred to in the second person). During the Middle Ages, everybody addressed everybody else in the second person, e.g.: *Hogy vagy?* (How are you?), and *Mióta vársz rám?* (How long have you been waiting for me?).

The non-second person addresses tied to the third person singular or plural came into fashion only in the 16th century. First to appear was the use of the formal pronoun *maga* (you), changing a reflexive pronoun into a personal pronoun, e.g.: *Maga is látta a balesetet?* (Did you also see the accident?), *Maga, István, hogyan tudna leghamarabb a repülőtérre érni?* (You, Stephen, how can you get to the airport the fastest way?), *Magához szólok* (I am speaking to you).

From this time on, one can see how the practice of using the second person and the third person diverged. The use of the second person suggested a confidential relationship between equals, while the third person form of address was between persons of different standing, more respectful and more distant. In the 19th century, largely on István Széchényi's recommendation, a new third person address became popular, using the pronoun *ön* (you) instead of *maga.* E.g.: *Önnel kettesben szeretnék moziba menni.* (I would like to go to the movies with you, just the two of us), *Ön olvasta ezt a cikket?* (Have you read this article?).

A third form uses the verb *tetszik* (does it please you, would you like), and is the most courteous of the three third person addresses, e.g.: *Le tetszik szállni?* (Are you getting off? - literally: Does it please you to be getting off), *Hogy tetszik lenni?* (How are you? - literally: How does it please you to be?).

It is a characteristic of the Hungarian language that the pronoun may even be omitted from the address, e.g.: *Julika, én szeretem önt!* / *Julika, én szeretem magát!* can be expressed as: *Julika, szeretem!* (In each case, the English translation is the same: "Julika, I love you!")

Today the use of the second person singular is considerably more widespread than it used to be. It is a general rule that this form of address must be suggested by the elder to the younger and by a woman to a man. Prior to World War II, married couples used the third person address to each other, and so did children toward their parents. Whether *maga* or *ön* was used varied from place to place and from age to age. Neither has a specific stylistic value and the choice was almost entirely *ad lib.* The *tetszik* form was used frequently when the speaker wanted to be particularly courteous or was unsure whether to use *maga* or *ön.*

Magának, elnök úr, mi a véleménye a pályázatomról?
(You, Mr. President, what do you think of my application?)

Önnek, elnök úr, mi a véleménye a pályázatomról?
(You, Mr. President, what do you think of my application?)

Hogyan tetszik elnök úrnak a pályázatom?
(How does my application please you, Mr. President?)

The hierarchical interpersonal relationships between the two World Wars are reflected by the so-called "gendarmes second person", i.e., the unilateral use of the second person address. Generally servants and low level employees were so addressed by employers and gendarmes used this form of address with the common people, to show their superiority. At the same time, there was a rigidly firm form of address depending on birth, class or position, which could not be violated. These were: *kegyelmes* (excellency), *méltóságos* (worshipful), *nagyságos* (gracious), and *tekintetes* (honorable). This completely changed after World War II, but there is one place where a remnant of the system still survives. In markets or stores one can still hear: *Nem kér egy kis almát, naccsád?* (Does the gracious lady want some apples?), *Van kegyednek szatyra?* (Does the honorable lady have a tote bag?). The loss of a more formal address is being partially – and necessarily – remedied by the use of *néni* and *bácsi* (aunt and uncle): *Leszáll a néni?* (Does the aunt get off?)

In Hungarian, greetings are related to the time of day: *Jó reggelt* (good morning), *Jó napot* (good day), *Jó estét* (good evening), and *Jó éjszakát* (good night). The word *kívánok* (I wish [you]) may be attached, but is not essential. To say good-by, *Viszontlátásra* (until we meet again) is always acceptable. Among friends who use the second person form of address, the word S*zervusz* (from the Latin *Servus humillimus* - your humble servant), is acceptable both as a greeting and at parting. Some of the young people have abbreviated this to *Szia* (perhaps from the English: see you!, but more probably an abbreviation of *szervusz*). Among the young, the greeting of *Hello, Hali,*

Ciao are now commonly used. Other, more personal forms of greeting, mostly among women, are: *Puszi* ([I] kiss [you]), *Pusz-Pusz* (kiss-kiss), *Csók* (kiss), *Csocsi* (kiss), and *Szióka* (a form of *Szia*).

In the country, the old, time-honored greetings are still used: *Adjon Isten (jó napot)* (God give you – a good day), *Isten hozta nálunk/errefelé* (God brought you to us/ this way). At departure: *Isten vele/magával* (God be with you). A common toast is: *Isten éltesse!* (God keep you.).

One of the curiosities of the Hungarian language is the form of address *Kezét csókolom* (I kiss your hand). This form of greeting arose at the Spanish Imperial Court and was taken over by the Viennese Court through their family relationships with the Spanish Imperial House. It was used not only in Vienna, but spread to all parts of the Monarchy (*Kisztihand, ruku libám, ruku boszkávam*), all meaning, I kiss your hand. With the dissolution of the Monarchy, this form of greeting disappeared everywhere, except in Hungary, where after World War II, it was considered an undesirable bourgeois rudiment. (Perhaps this is why it hung on.) And so, today a polite gentleman will still greet a lady with *Kezét csókolom* (or just *Csókolom*). Children use this form for any adult and, while it is a relatively recent arrival, this form of greeting is now quite popular in the rural districts as well.

The Hungarian forms of greeting and address are highly intricate. They still maintain a certain feudal echo, show the earlier break in the bourgeois culture, and also demonstrate the equalizing effects of socialism. There is nothing really standard about it, and occasionally the well-meant courtesy may prove to be offensive.

The Hungarian Language Today: Character and Trends

Changes in the language become noticeable first by changes in the vocabulary. Noticing grammatical and phonetic changes requires considerable study. For this reason, in showing the character and trends of the current Hungarian language I will first show the changes in the vocabulary and only then the grammatical and phonetic changes and the changes indicative of the changing times.

Frequent word combinations:

In earlier times, the most frequent form of expanding the vocabulary and creating new words consisted of synthesizing suffix usage. During the past few decades, this method took second place and word combinations became more popular, e.g.: *sétálóutca* (walking/pedestrian street), *körgyűrű* (beltway – boulevard), *ezermesterbolt* (literally: Jack of all trades shop, home repairs shop), *újszíves* (somebody ill with heart disease). There appeared also some excessively long words, the so-called "sea-monster words," which clearly offend against the esthetics of the language, e.g.: *szociálisalap-hiány* (lack of [moneys] for the social safety-net), *településrendezés-program* (a program to regulate housing developments). These can be replaced by a multi-word description.

Live word formation:

In view of the richness in verbal and nominal suffixes, the role of new word formation in the Hungarian language is still a significant one. Some quite newly formed words which have not even made it to the dictionary are: *hiénázik* (literally: makes like a hyena - eats leftovers in a cafeteria), *forintosít* (expresses values in forints), *szexel* (has intercourse), *parasztizál* (does peasant work), and *gyárista* (factory worker). Diminutive suffixes may also be attached to almost any noun to make new words in everyday speech, e.g.: *édes - éd-i* (sweet - cute), *doktor - dok-i* (doctor - doc), *finom - fincsi* (good - yummi), etc.

Word shortening - "turbo-speech":

Shortening words seems to be a general trend in all languages. It may be related to the accelerating patterns of life and to the general tendency to speak faster. We can see this in Hungarian as well: *irtózatos → irtó* (dreadful), *tulajdonos → tulaj* (owner), *laboratórium → labor* (laboratory), *bizományi vállalat → bizó* (commission enterprise), *jugoszláv → jugó* (Yugoslav), *trolibusz → troli* (trolley-bus), and *baromi jó → baró* (damned good). This is further complemented by the addition of a diminutive suffix *i* to the already abbreviated words: *cukrászda → cuki* (pastry shop), *cigaretta → cigi* (cigarette), *proletár → proli* (proletarian), *hamburger → hambi* (hamburger), *McDonald's → meki* (McDonald's), *villamos → vili* (street car), *prostituált → prosti* (prostitute), *homoszexuális → homi* (gay), *-ó → pletyka - pletyó* (gossip), *táska - tatyó* (hand bag), *-ci → történelem - törci* (history), *futball - foci* (soccer), *-csi- finom - fincsi* (good, yummy), *dollár → dolcsi* (dollar).

The grocers use *-i* diminutives to record produce prices in their stores. E.g.: *saláta → sali* (salad), *mogyoró → mogyi* (hazelnut), *paradicsom → pari* (tomato), and *fokhagyma → foki* (garlic).

There are also word abbreviations where in a compound elements get shortened and a new word stands for the whole compound: E.g.: *mozgóképszínház → mozi* (motion picture theater, popularized by writer Jenő Heltai), *magánszektor → maszek* (private sector, created by the humorist Dezső Kellér in the 1950s), *ebédszünet → ebszün* (lunch break), *denaturált szesz → denszesz* (denatured alcohol), *viszontlátásra → viszlát* (good-by), *repülőtér → reptér* (airport), *fizetési mérleg → fizmérleg* (payment balance).

Mosaic words (acronyms):

The shortest words are the words constructed from the initial letters of several words. The Hungarians call the supermarkets *"Közért"*, although few of them know that the word is derived from *Községi* Élelmiszer*értékesítő* Vállalat (Municipal Food Sales and Distribution Company). Another grocery chain is known as *ABC*, which is the acronym for *A*lapvető *B*olti *C*ikkek (Basic Store Items).

Foreign words, "Hunglish":

A frequently used method for increasing the vocabulary is to borrow words from another language. Foreign words enter the present Hungarian language in a continuous stream. Earlier these were German words, but lately the largest number of words come from the English. We can speak of Hunglish (Hungarian-English) words which have entered our language recently.

According to an international study most of the borrowed **English word**s refer to the entertainment industry, followed by business and then by the scientific, technical vocabulary. The following have been generally accepted into the Hungarian language: *baby-sitter, bojkott, hurrá, huligán, lincs, löncs, makadám, morze, kardigán, pulóver, szendvics, szex* and *futball.* (No translation is necessary. The words are obvious in spite of the Magyarized spelling.)

Some more recent words or expressions from English are: *bodizik* (he's doing, is engaged in body building), *bébi, marketing, music center, talk show, image, menedzserkalkulátor.*

Many words pertain to the mass media and to computer science (*mono, sztereo, DAT-magnó, CD-játszó* [player], *szoftver, hardver, winchester, diszk, file*), sports (*body-building, jet-ski, kick-box, windsurf, snow-board*), enterprise or store names (*diszkó, second hand shop, solarium, night club, hot dog, snack bar, peep show, music center, megastore*), economy and finance (*leasing - lízing, tender,*

173

outplacement, marketing, bróker, disztributor, image), and politics (*lobbi* and *ombudsman*), have all been taken over from the English language. Some English words are adapted to the Hungarian language to the point where they take on Hungarian suffixes: *diszkózik* (he frequents a disco), *lobbizik* (he engages in lobbying), *szörföl/szörföz* (he engages in surfing).

In the 1930s there was a strong tendency to Magyarize the language of sports, particularly soccer. Today the terminology of the newer sports is all in English and even Far-Eastern sport terms have come to us through English. We also see a certain reversal, back to English. Instead of *kocogás* we now tend to say *jogging*, for *edző* we use *tréner*, for *gyúró, masszőr,* for *cselgáncs, dzsúdó*.

Helló, OK, all right and *sorry* are used commonly in present day Hungarian. The growing prestige of American culture can be seen in the fact that movie distributors frequently use the original English title of a movie, e.g.: *Jurassic Park*. Hungarian periodicals are given English names: *Cinema, Flex, Fitness*. In some want ads the job is indicated only in English: *sales manager*.

In some structures we can recognize the influence of English. E.g.: *nem igazán* (not really), *ez nem ilyen egyszerű* (It's not so simple), *Legyen egy jó napjuk* (Let's have a good day - enjoy ourselves), *Jó délutánt* (good afternoon).

Unusual new verbal suffixes:

On the basis of analogy and through the effect of some dialects, peculiar verbal suffixes have come into use. In the first person singular of the conditional tense, instead of *-nék, -nák* has appeared in a few words, though this usage is not considered proper, e.g.: *olvasnák egy könyvet* (I would like to read a book) or *itt szívesebben laknák* (I would prefer to live here) instead of the traditional *olvasnék* and *laknék*. In a way this follows the rule of tonality, which would endorse this usage even though it is contrary to previous usage. Another related phenomenon applies

174

to verbs ending in *-t* or *-szt,* where the imperative form is used incorrectly in lieu of the declarative form: *kifessük a lakást,* instead of: *kifestjük* a lakást (we paint the apartment), and *a munkát elhalasszuk,* instead of *a munkát elhalasztjuk* (we postpone the work).

Analytic trend:
The analytic (divisive) manifestations are increasing in the Hungarian language. This is also one of the results of the postpositions. New postpositions appear all the time, e.g: *alkalommal* (on the occasion of), *céljából* (for the purpose of), *értelmében* (in the sense of), *tekintetében* (with respect to), *alapján* (on the basis of), *során* (as a consequence of), *terén* (on the basis of). These generally lead to unnecessary excess verbiage (which we call verbal sprawl): *A könyveladás tekintetében csökkent a bevétel* (With respect to the sale of books, the income has decreased). More simply and correctly: *A könyveladásban csökken a bevétel* (Income has decreased in the sale of books). A postposition was used for what a suffix could express adequately. Single verbs are being replaced by verbal constructions, e.g.: instead of *elintéz* (takes care of) they say: *elintézést nyer* (it achieves being taken care of), and instead of *megvizsgál* (examines) they say: *vizsgálat tárgyává lesz* (it will become the subject of an examination). This verbal sprawl is partly due to Indo-European influences.

Reversed attribute construction:
Under the influence of the Indo-European languages, reverse attribute constructions have appeared in the Hungarian language. The usual sequence is attribute+qualified word. In the reverse structure we find qualified word+attribute: *Ford Népliget* (Ford park), *Rádió Esztergom* (Radio Esztergom), *M1-es (autópálya)* (Motorway #1).

Emphasis:
The old Hungarian rules of emphasis no longer apply in all cases. Perhaps under Indo-European influence, the end of the sentence is prolonged and left dangling. The traditional emphasis on the first word keeps sliding further backward. *Mit vár ettől az eseménytől?* (What do you expect from this event?), *Hány órakor kezdődik az előadás?* (At what time does the performance begin?). The speakers perhaps believe that the verb is a more important part of the sentence than the subject and that the qualified word carries more weight than the attribute. This may be true for the German language but it certainly is not true for Hungarian. In fact, the shift in emphasis may lead to misunderstanding or make a joke of the sentence. E.g.: Somebody asks the concierge of the Ministry: *Hányan dolgoznak a minisztériumban?* (How many people work in the Ministry?). But this could also be taken as: How many people do any work in the Ministry? if *dolgoznak* is stressed.

Turbo-speak and pronounciation:
The increased tempo of ordinary speech can be observed in the increase in gabbling and in swallowing syllables. The former party leadership could never pronounce *szocializmus* properly and always said: *szoc'lizmus*. In the military, *százados úr* (captain) is now pronounced *száz'úr*. Another example for swallowing syllables: *Kel'm Csaba á't'isk'ai tan'ló* for: *Kelemen Csaba általános iskolai tanuló* (Kelemen Csaba, public school student).

Dropping letters:
A slower speaking tempo, the so-called "Kádár speech", was particularly noticeable in political speeches. The dropping of letters reflected the excessive respect for the written word that characterized the Socialist political system. Thus, the politicians read adjacent consonants phonetically and created sounds that differed widely from the spo-

ken language and revealed a fundamental lack of education. E.g.: *ad-ják* (they give), *tud-ja* (he knows), *a szocializmus út-ján* (on the path of Socialism), rather than the correct *aggyák, tuggya,* and *úttyán*).

New consonant combinations: In the past, the Hungarian language did away with consonant clusters, which were generally foreign to the Finno-Ugrian languages. Today, however, the Hungarian speakers are not bothered by such forms as: *sztratoszféra* (stratosphere) and *sztriptíz* (strip tease).

Hungarian in the Global Village

The words derived from the Hungarian language demonstrate the political, economic, cultural and intellectual ties between people and between languages. Over the centuries a strange peregrination of words has taken place. Many words from the Hungarian governmental, legal, religious, military and economic vocabulary were taken over by the neighboring Slavic languages and by Romanian. E.g.: *ország* (country), *város* (city), *nádorispán* (Palatine), *vármegye* (county), *peres* (disputed), *tudomány* (science), *folyás* (conduct), *tanács* (advice, council), *tábor* (camp), *sereg* (army), *sátor* (tent), *szoba* (room), *bíró* (judge), *juhász* (shepherd), *hintó* (carriage), *szállás* (lodgings), *hadnagy* (lieutenant), *vám* (customs), *gazda* (master, owner).

A number of words assumed to be of Slavic origin have been transformed in Hungarian and were then returned in their new form to the Slavic languages. E.g.: *akó* (an old measure of capacity), *asztal* (table), *csárda* (tavern), *kormány* (government), *parlag* (fallow), *sánta* (lame), and *vajda* (voivode). The Hungarian *-ó* suffix can be seen in the Croatian language: *lopó - lopov* (gourd), and has contributed to other Slavic words: *lazov* (liar), *nitkov* (a nobody). Hungarian words also appear as mirror images in various Slavic languages. E.g.: *házasság* (marriage), *házastárs* (marriage partner), *lelkiismeret* (conscience), and *írástudó* (scribe, clerk).

There is also a Hungarian vocabulary that has been taken over by the great European and world languages. We may term these as literary words of Hungarian origin. They are words of "Hungarian romanticism" or even "*Puszta* (prairie) romanticism". This went to the point where in the 1970s, western politicians referred to the Hungarian type of socialism as *Goulash Communism*. By this they meant that the leaders of the country had set Communist goals, but were running a country whose socialist organizations differed from the surrounding areas and where there was plenty to eat and drink, even though some other things may be in short supply.

The word *kocsi,* which exists in some form in most languages, is also of Hungarian origin. Kocs is the name of a Transdanubian village, and it is from this village that the world famous carriage originates. *Kocsi (kocs-i)* literally means something coming from Kocs. The Hungarian *kocsi* (carriage) was a light, wooden construction, suspended and thus swaying while under way (swaying in Hungarian is *hinta,* and hence another name for a gentleman's carriage in Hungary is *hintó,* i.e., something that sways). The *kocsi* made it possible to travel in great comfort. The Spanish historian Avila y Zuniga was also aware of the *kocsi.* In his *Commentarios de la guerra de Alemana hecha por Carlos V, en 1546 y 1547* (Commentaries of the war made by Charles V in Germany in 1546 and 1547) he writes about the travel of the Emperor, who was tormented by gout: "Charles V was sleeping in a covered carriage which is known in Hungary as a *kocsi* and the name and the invention originate in that country."

Today, the word *kocsi* has come to be the shortened version of *gépkocsi,* i.e., motorcar, car. E.g.: *Vettem egy kocsit* (I have bought a car), and *Elromlott a kocsim* (My car is broken down).

Another international word which originated from Hungary is *hajdú* (Heyduck). The first mention comes from 1514 and at that time the word meant cattle herdsman. The word *hajdú* is derived from the Hungarian word *hajt* which means driving. The *hajdúk* (or *hajtók*) drove cattle from Hungary to Austria, Germany and Italy. A comment from 1553 refers to a *hajdútánc* (hajdu dance). The *hajdúk* were tough, battle ready men since they had to defend their cattle against all comers. István Bocskai, the Prince of Transylvania, formed them into a military outfit, gave them the privileges of nobility, and settled them on his own estates. In Eastern-Hungary there is a County Hajdú, and there are numerous place names incorporating the word: *Hajdúszoboszló, Hajdúböszörmény, Hajdúdorog,* etc. Later on the name was used for the law enforcement officials of the counties and towns, who wore particularly ornate braided uniforms. The word *hajdú* was taken over by many other languages. In German it is *Heiduck* (a uniformed non-commissioned officer), in French *heiduque* (Hungarian infantry man), in Italian *aiduco,* in Serb and Croatian *hajduk,* in Russian *gajduk* (freedom fighter, bandit, highway robber), in Romanian *haiduc* and in Turkish *haydut* (robber).

The Hungarian *huszár* is also an international word which originally reached Hungary from the Byzantine Greek, via Serb and Croatian. It was in Hungarian that it assumed the meaning of a light cavalry soldier and it was this meaning that spread later to the other European languages. It is *hussar* in English, *hussard* in French, *ussaro* in Italian, *guszar* in Russian and *huzaar* in Dutch.

The *sujtás* (linear braiding) found on the uniforms of the *hajdúk* and *hussars* also reached a number of European languages. It is *soutache* in English, *Schoitasch* in German, *soutache* in French and *soitas* in Romanian. The same thing happened to the word *mulatság* (entertainment) that is known in Germany and in the United States. The word *csákó* originally meant the horns of cattle that were curved vertically upward. Yet, in 1729 we have a written memorial that reads: *"Minden katonának csákós süvege légyen."* (Let every soldier have a *csákó*-like high cap). Apparently, this was a high hat with two pointed corners in some way reminiscent of the characteristic horns of Hungarian cattle. The word spread to other languages. It is *shako* in English, *Tschako* in German, *chako* in French and *czako* in Polish.

The traditional name for the Hungarian Great Plains cattle herders is *gulyás*. The excellent thick soup dish cooked by them in open kettles was also known as *gulyás-leves* (gulyás soup). The English *goulash*, the German *Gulasch*, the French *goulache*, the Finn *gulassi* and the Dutch *goulash* are all derived from the Hungarian. And last but not least, the Hungarian type of communism received the nickname of "gulyás (goulash) communism".

The Hungarian *puszta* is an extensive, sandy, alkaline flat area in the Hungarian Great Plains (Alföld). It serves even today as a breeding area for horses and cattle under conditions similar to the range country in the United States. The most famous Hungarian *pusztas* and the centers of the *puszta* romanticism are Bugac and Hortobágy. The word puszta has also become an international one. It is *puszta* in English, *Pussta* in German, *pusta* in Slovakian, *pusztinya* in Russian and *poesta* in Dutch. The outcasts of society used to live on the *puszta* and in the forests and were known as *betyárs* (brigands, highwaymen). The most famous ones were Jóska Sobri, Jóska Savanyú, Marci Vidróczki and Sándor Rózsa. They were hunted down toward the middle of the 19th century but their memory was kept alive in *betyár* stories and ballads. The word *betyár* has gone into several languages from the original Hungarian. It is *Betjar* in German and *betár* in Slovakian. The name of the Hungarian dance, the *csárdás,* is also well known world-wide and so is the *tokaji aszú* (a famous wine), the *paprika* from Szeged and Kalocsa, and the *barackpálinka* (apricot brandy) from Kecskemét. The English term *biro* for a ball point pen is derived from the name of László Bíró, who invented this indispensable writing instrument.

We have now reached the end of our journey of discovery, and we hope that we have succeeded in helping the reader to some insights into the nature and workings of Hungarian – an intriguing non-Indo-European language spoken in the heart of Europe.

The Chronology of the Hungarian Language

B.C.

6000 - 4000	the Uralic "ethnic family"; Uralic-Altaic "ethnic family"
4000 - 2000	the Finno-Ugrian ethnic family
2000 - 1500	Ugors, Ur-Hungarians
1000	ancient Hungarian language; birth of an independent Hungarian language

A.D.

c. 400	the Huns in the Carpathian Basin
463	Levédia, the first "reconstructed" ancient Hungarian homeland
567	Avars in the Carpathian Basin
c. 670	White Ogurs in the Carpathian Basin
895 - 6	the (last) conquest, headed by Árpád
1000 (after)	beginning of Hungarian writing using the Latin alphabet
1055	the Tihany Charter with 58 Hungarian words
1192 - 5	Funerary Oration and Prayer
1200 (before)	the Königsberg Fragment
1235 - 7	Brother Julianus in Magna Hungaria
1260 - 70	the Gyulafehérvár Lines
c. 1300	the Ancient Hungarian Lamentation of Mary (first poem in Hungarian)
1372 - 1400	the Jókai Codex (first Hungarian manuscript, or continuous codex)
1434 - 72	Janus Pannonius, the first Hungarian poet (wrote in Latin)
1450 - 1500	the Hussite Bible (first Hungarian translation of the Bible)
1471	first printing shop opened in Buda

1490	Sopron Flower Song (first folksong noted down)
1539	the first Hungarian grammar
1590	the first Protestant Bible (Gáspár Károlyi, Vizsoly)
1590 (after)	birth of Hungarian literary language
1608	Albert Szenczi Molnár's grammar for foreigners
1685	Miklós Misztótfalusi Kis: the Golden Bible (Amsterdam)
1770 - 1870	reformation of the Hungarian language
1772	beginning of the Enlightenment
1832	the Academy of Sciences publishes the first handbook of Hungarian spelling
1844	Hungarian becomes the official language
1870 (after)	Ugrian-Turkic "war" on the origins of the Hungarian language
1896	the Millennium (the 1000th anniversary of Hungarian statehood)
1938	foundation of the World Federation of Hungarians
1989	declaration of the Hungarian Republic (October 23)
1992	foundation of Duna Television
1996	Millecentennial (the 1100th anniversary of the Hungarian Conquest)
2000	second millennium of Hungarian statehood

Bibliography

Comprehensive Works

Géza Bárczi, *A magyar nyelv életrajza* (Biography of the Hungarian Language), Gondolat, Budapest, 1963.

Géza Bárczi, Lóránd Benkő and Jolán Berrár, *A magyar nyelv története* (History of the Hungarian language), Tankönyvkiadó, Budapest, 1967.

Lóránd Benkő and Samu Imre, ed., *The Hungarian Language,* Akadémiai, Budapest, 1972.

Gyula Décsy, *Die linguistische Struktur Europas* (The linguistic structure of Europe), Wiesbaden, 1973.

Péter Hajdú - Péter Domokos, *Uráli nyelvrokonaink* (Our Uralian Linguistic Relatives), Tankönyvkiadó, Budapest, 1978.

Jenő Kiss, *"A magyar nyelv"* (The Hungarian Language), 77-161. In: *A magyarságtudomány kézikönyve,* ed. László Kósa. Akadémiai, Budapest, 1991.

Endre Rácz, ed., *A mai magyar nyelv* (The Hungarian Language Today), Tankönyvkiadó, Budapest, 1968.

Sándor Rot, *Hungarian - Its Origin and Originality,* Korona Publishing House, Budapest, 1994.

Basic Dictionaries

László T. András - Zoltán Kövecses, *Magyar-angol szlengszótár* (Hungarian - English Thesaurus of Slang), Maecenas, Budapest, 1989, and *Angol-magyar szlengszótár* (English - Hungarian Dictionary of Slang), Eötvös Kiadó, 1994.

Lóránd Benkő ed., *A magyar nyelv történeti-etimológiai szótára* (The Historical and Etymological Dictionary of the Hungarian Language), I-III, Akadémia, Budapest, 1967-1976.

Gergely Czuczor - János Fogarasi, *A magyar nyelv szótára* (Dictionary of the Hungarian Language), I-IV, Pest, 1862-1874.

Miklós Hernádi, *Közhelyszótár* (Dictionary of Clichés),
Gondolat, Budapest, 1984, 1995.
Lajos Kiss, *Földrajzi nevek etimológiai szótára* (Etymological
Dictionary of Geographic Names), I-II, Akadémiai,
Budapest, 1988.
Magyar Értelmező Kéziszótár (Hungarian Explanatory Concise
Dictionary). Akadémiai, Budapest, 1972.

Reference Works

Géza Balázs - László Marácz, *"Nyelvgeopolitika"* (Linguistic
Geo-Politics). In: *Magyar Nyelvőr,* 1995, 31-47.
János Gulya, *"A magyar nyelv finnugor sajátosságai"*
(Finno-Ugrian Characteristics of the Hungarian Language),
37-42. In: *A finnugor tudományágak és a tudományos
ismeretterjesztés* (Finno-Ugrian Sciences and Scientific
Education), ed. Gulya János, TIT, Budapest, 1976.
Imre Katona, *"A magyar néptörténet modellje"* (A Model for
Hungarian Popular History). In: *Anthropologiai
Közlemények,* 1987/88, 143-147.
Jenő Kiss, *Magyar anyanyelvűek - a magyar nyelvhasználat*
(Hungarian Native Speakers - Hungarian Usage), Nemzeti
Tankönyvkiadó, Budapest, 1994.
István Kiszely, *A magyarság őstörténete. (Mit adott a magyarság a
világnak?)* (Hungarian Ancient History - What have the
Hungarians given to the World?), I-II, Püski, Budapest, 1996.
Gyula László, *Őstörténetünk* (Our Ancient History), 3rd ed.,
Tankönyvkiadó, Budapest, 1987.
Gyula László, *The Magyars. Their Life and Civilisation,* Corvina,
Budapest, 1996.
László Marácz, Hongaarse kentering, Aspekt, Utrecht, 1995. –
Hungarian Revival. Aspekt, Utrecht, 1996.
Jerry Payne, *Colloquial Hungarian,* Routledge, 1987.
János Pusztay, *Az "ugor-török" háború után* (After the "Ugrian-
Turkish" War), Gyorsuló Idő, Magvető, Budapest, 1977.
Géza Varga, ed., *Bronzkori magyar írásbeliség* (Bronze-age
Hungarian Writing), Írástörténeti Kutató Intézet, Budapest,
1993.

Index

Printed in Hungary , 1997